LEARN SQUASH
AND RACQUETBALL
IN A WEEKEND

LEARN SQUASH
AND RACQUETBALL
IN A WEEKEND

JAHANGIR KHAN
with KEVIN PRATT

Photography by Matthew Ward

ALFRED A. KNOPF
New York
1993

A DORLING KINDERSLEY BOOK

Art Editor Alison Donovan
Editor Deborah Opoczynska
Senior Art Editor Amanda Lunn
Series Editors Jo Weeks, Laura Harper
Deputy Art Director Tina Vaughan
Deputy Editorial Director Jane Laing
Production Controller Helen Creeke

First published in Great Britain in 1993
by Dorling Kindersley Limited,
9 Henrietta Street, London WC2E 8PS

Library of Congress Cataloging-in-Publication Data

Khan. Jahangir.
  Learn squash and racquetball in a weekend / by Jahangir Khan.
    p. cm.
  ISBN 0-679-42753-8
  1. Squash rackets (Game)
  2. Racquetball. I. Title.
GV1004.K47 1993
796.34'3--dc20   93-16704
                                    CIP

Computer page make-up by Cloud 9
Designs, UK. Reproduced by Colourscan,
Singapore. Printed and bound
by Arnoldo Mondadori, Verona, Italy

CONTENTS

INTRODUCTION

SQUASH IS MY LIFE. Ever since I was a boy in Pakistan, all I have wanted to do is hit that little ball around the court. I came to England and set out to fulfill my ambition: to become the best player in the world. In 1981, when I was 17, my dream came true: I won the World Open Final against my old rival, Geoff Hunt. From there, I went on to maintain the longest unbeaten run in the history of the game – five years, seven months, and one day. After many years at the pinnacle of my sport, I still love playing squash; there is always something new to learn in practice, there is always a new limit to aim for in training, and there is always a new challenge with every opponent. The rules are easy to learn and you can very quickly start playing enjoyable, competitive games with players of your own standard. If you join a club, you will be able to take part in competitions and improve

THE WINNER
Winner of ten British Opens, six World Championships, and numerous other competitions throughout the globe, Jahangir Khan will go down in history as the best squash player of all time.

your ability by taking on players of higher standards. This book shows you how to master the rudiments of the game over the course of a weekend, right from the basics of hitting the ball correctly, through the subtleties of match-winning technique to the exercise it takes to acquire the necessary level of fitness. It will also serve as an invaluable source of reference as you hone your squash skills in the years to come. There are now 15 million people around the world who play regularly, so you are about to learn one of the most popular sports of the day. I hope this book sets you on the path toward a life-long love of squash. No matter what your age, if you are enthusiastic and apply a little dedication, you are sure to be enriched both physically and mentally by this wonderful game.

JAHANGIR KHAN

PREPARING FOR THE WEEKEND

Get the most from your Weekend Course by preparing in advance

YOU WILL LEARN MORE, and have greater fun, if you plan your weekend in advance. Arrange to have a court at your disposal by hiring one from a local club or recreation center. If possible, find a partner who is as keen to learn as you are. Make sure you have the right equipment, including proper squash shoes, clothing, racket, and balls. Take up a fitness program before you start playing. There is an old squash saying that is worth remembering: "Get fit to play squash; don't play squash to get fit". Study the rules of the game (see p.17) so that you have a basic understanding of how squash is played before you even set foot on the court. Familiarize yourself with the court markings and the basic positions, such as where to serve from, where to receive the serve, and where to stand during a **rally**. Get used to holding your racket with the

SQUASH WEAR
Invest in good-quality clothing, including on-court wear and a tracksuit. Sneakers or tennis shoes are no substitute for a good pair of squash shoes.

• *Choose the speed of ball suited to you*

• *Buy proper squash shoes*

• *Store equipment in a gym bag*

RACKETS & BALLS
Find a racket that feels just right for you – neither too heavy nor too light. Make sure the grip is comfortable. Buy a selection of fast and slow balls, so that you can determine which is best suited to your style of play.

Make sure the grip is comfortable •

Use wraps to make the grip more secure •

YOU WILL LEARN MORE, and have greater fun, if you plan your weekend in advance. Arrange to have a court at your disposal by hiring one from a local club or recreation center. If possible, find a partner who is as keen to learn as you are. Make sure you have the right equipment, including proper squash shoes, clothing, racket, and balls. Take up a fitness program before you start playing. There

(32ft (9.7m))

5ft 2in (1.6m)

14ft (4.3m)

21ft (6.4m)

5ft 5in (1.7m)

• Learn the rules about swings

COURT DIMENSIONS
You will be able to develop a good feel for the dimensions of a squash court simply by walking around one. Take some time to watch how the other players position themselves and move around the court while playing.

RULES OF THE GAME
Learn the rules about **obstruction** and illegal racket swings. This will help to ensure that you have a safe and enjoyable game, and that you do not lose it merely through default.

• Look straight ahead

WARMING UP ON-COURT
Go through a number of exercises on the court to thoroughly warm your muscles. This will help you to avoid any muscle injuries and soreness.

• Concentrate on moving smoothly

WARMING UP OFF-COURT
Before you set foot on the court, ensure that your muscles are prepared for the game by taking up regular exercise in a gym or other spacious area.

• Exercise to improve strength and stamina

SQUASH KIT

"Dress well, play well" is a good rule for squash players to follow

SQUASH IS A FAST AND VIGOROUS GAME, not a fashion parade, but it is important to have the right attitude to your gym clothes. By playing in shabby or dirty clothes, you are showing a lack of respect for your opponent, for yourself, and for the sport. Smart, clean clothes show your regard for the game and that you are taking matters seriously. Shorts, skirts, and shirts must be able to stretch to allow you to reach for the ball; avoid materials that soak up perspiration. Keep a towel on-court to dry yourself. Put money and valuables in your gym bag and place it close to the front wall. It is essential to wear a good pair of squash shoes to help movement and reduce the risk of slips and injury.

OFF-COURT WEAR

What you wear before and after your game is almost as important as what you wear on-court. Warm ups will prevent you getting cold while you loosen your muscles before playing, and while you warm down after the game. You may choose to wear your warmup to the court, but don't put it back on over your squash clothes after playing – wet clothes will give you a chill. Never wear your squash shoes off the court – it ruins the sole.

• **MATERIAL**
Choose a warmup made of a flexible, warm material, that allows you to ease and stretch muscles without the risk of "cold-start" injuries.

WARMUP
Always wear your warmup to loosen up in before starting the game. This helps to avoid injuries on-court and unnecessary stiffness the day after.

GYM BAG
Buy a large bag with compartments for valuables, clothes, wet towels, toiletries, rackets, and balls.

ON-COURT WEAR

Clothes should be comfortable and
clean, to help you feel fresh and ready
for a good game. Wear light colors so
that the ball stands out clearly against
you. Remove any items of jewelry
that might cause
injury to yourself
or, more likely,
to your opponent.
Only put your
squash shoes on
once on the court.

• SHIRT
A short-sleeved shirt
with an open neck allows
freedom of movement.
Wear it neatly tucked in.

SHORTS •
A fast game of squash
involves many strides
and leaps. Wear shorts
that stretch to avoid
embarrassing splits.

• SKIRTS
Women should wear skirts
that allow easy movement,
but are long enough to deter
any unwanted scrutiny.

UNDERWEAR
Underwear is important if
you are to be comfortable
on-court. Men should wear
a support, and women will
need a well-fitting sports
bra. Unsuitable garments
may cause discomfort and
distract you from the game.

• SOCKS
Good socks protect against blisters.
Avoid cheap or ill-fitting pairs that
will aggravate weakened skin.

SHOES

The correct shoes are essential. Invest in
a pair of squash shoes, rather than relying
on standard sneakers or tennis shoes. The
grip, heel, and ankle support are different
on a squash shoe and make a significant
difference in terms of performance as well
as of the risk of injury. Make sure the soles
of the shoes are non-marking. Wear new
shoes around the house to break them in
and help to avoid blisters. Tie laces so that
they never touch the ground, otherwise
you are quite likely to trip and fall.

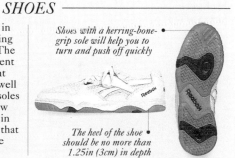

*Shoes with a herring-bone-
grip sole will help you to
turn and push off quickly*

*The heel of the shoe •
should be no more than
1.25in (3cm) in depth*

RACKETS & BALLS

Choose the ball and racket that feel best for you

GREAT ADVANCES HAVE BEEN MADE in squash-racket technology. Originally made of wood with animal-gut strings, there was little to distinguish one racket from another, but today's rackets are made of graphite with synthetic strings and have various shaped heads. They can present a bewildering choice to the beginner. There are four types of ball, each suited to different levels and styles of play.

RACKETS

Choose a racket that feels right. If it is cumbersome, it is too heavy. If it feels like a feather, it is too light. Try out several until you shake hands with the one for you. The most expensive racket is a waste of money at this stage, since only a good player can take advantage of it. The cheapest ones are made of inferior materials, and can smash easily. Ask other players what they recommend.

VIBRATION
A great force is generated when you strike the ball and some of it shoots down the racket and into your arm. A **vibration absorber** (above), placed in the center of the racket face, helps to lessen this effect.

Vibration absorber

Small round head •

• Large oval head

HEAD •
Regardless of the size of the head, the best way to hit the ball is in the center of the racket face. A larger head is not necessarily an advantage, but may provide the beginner with extra confidence.

SHAFT •
Graphite rackets are stronger than wood, which is important when you hit the wall instead of the ball, but the shaft is still vulnerable, so avoid undue strain.

Open-throat head •

• STRINGS
When racket strings break, they can easily be replaced. Some players insist on gut because it gives more "spin", but it is not as hard-wearing as nylon.

prince

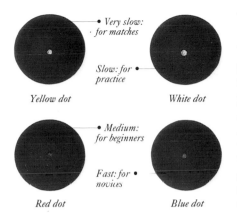

• Very slow: for matches

Slow: for practice

Yellow dot

White dot

• Medium: for beginners

Fast: for novices •

Red dot

Blue dot

BALLS

Squash balls are hollow. When used, they become warm and the air inside expands, making them more bouncy. The better you are, the slower the ball you should use. If you use a ball that is too fast to start off with, it will become so bouncy that good squash becomes impossible. Use the blue- and red-dot balls to begin with; you can graduate to the white and yellow ones as you begin to gain confidence.

RACKET COVERS

Most rackets come with a cover, but buy one if yours did not. The cover will prevent the frame from being scuffed and the strings from breakage. It will also protect your racket against the elements – rain, which damages strings, and excessive cold, which can seriously weaken the shaft.

SECURITY
The best place to keep your squash rackets and balls is in your cover. For security, attach your name and address to it in case you lose it.

• Single-racket cover

• Multi-racket bag

GRIPS

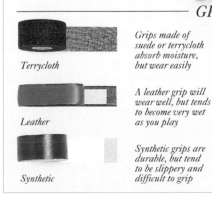

Terrycloth

Grips made of suede or terrycloth absorb moisture, but wear easily

Leather

A leather grip will wear well, but tends to become very wet as you play

Synthetic

Synthetic grips are durable, but tend to be slippery and difficult to grip

Rackets have suede, terrycloth, leather, or synthetic grips. Suede and terry grips absorb moisture but wear easily. Leather wears well but can become wet as you perspire. Synthetics are also long-lasting but tend to have a slippery surface and can fly out of your hand, which is very dangerous for your opponent. Whichever grip you use, make sure it is dry. Always use a towel between points to keep your hands dry. If your hands are big, build up the size of the handle with taping. There should be a 0.5in (1cm) gap between your fingers and your palm when you grip the handle.

COURT DIMENSIONS

It is vital to become familiar with the field of battle

A SQUASH COURT CAN SEEM QUITE SMALL, until you have to start racing from one end of it to the other in order to reach the ball. The secret of the game, therefore, is to force your opponent out of position, while remaining in a dominant position yourself. Spend a few minutes walking around the court in order to familiarize yourself with the distances and angles that exist in this unique area.

32ft (9.7m)
Out line

MARKINGS

The red court-markings are found on the walls and floor. They define both where to stand when serving and the areas within which you are allowed to hit the ball. The serve, the first shot in any game, must hit the front wall above the **cut line**, before hitting any other wall. It must then rebound past the **short line** and into the receiver's box, before it hits the floor. If the ball does not reach the receiver's box, or if the ball goes above the **out lines** or into the **tin**, the server loses the **rally**.

7ft (2.1m)

32ft (9.7m)

5ft 3in (1.6m)

14ft (4.3m)

5ft 5in (1.7m)

21ft (6.4m)

FLOOR MARKINGS
You must have one foot in the service box when you are serving. If you win the point off your serve, you swap to the opposite box with each serve thereafter until you lose the **rally**, when the serve passes to your opponent. The junction between the **short line** and the **half-court** line forms the T, the central area that is of supreme, strategic importance.

WALL MARKINGS

The ball is "out" if it hits above any of the **out lines** or goes into the **tin**. A shot is also counted "out" if the ball hits the line itself.

DIMENSIONS

The principal target area is the front wall, measuring 15ft (4.6m) high and 21ft (6.4m) wide. The court is 32ft (9.7m) deep, with a full diagonal of 38ft 3in (11.7m). The side walls slope down to 7ft (2.1m), the height of the back wall playing area. All serves must reach above the **cut line** – 6ft (1.8m) above the floor.

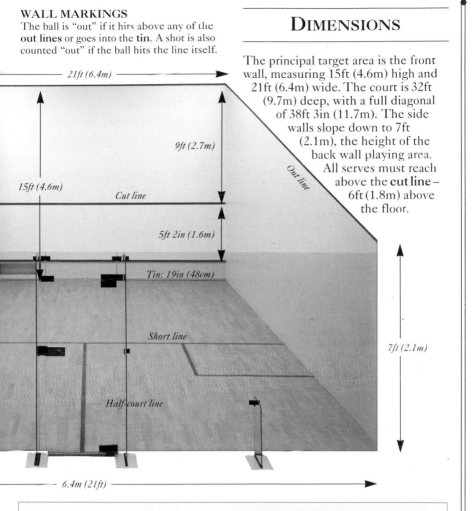

21ft (6.4m)

9ft (2.7m)

15ft (4.6m)

Cut line

Out line

5ft 2in (1.6m)

Tin: 19in (48cm)

Short line

7ft (2.1m)

Half-court line

6.4m (21ft)

TELECOURT

The rise in popularity of squash in recent years has increased demand for spectator facilities at the major championships. Glass "goldfish bowl" courts have been developed that act like a one-way mirror so that the audience can see in from all four sides of the arena, but the players cannot see out. Adaptations have also been made to allow the television cameras to capture the excitement of the fast-moving sport, with special squash balls that are picked up clearly by the cameras.

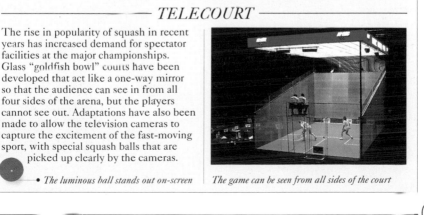

• *The luminous ball stands out on-screen*

The game can be seen from all sides of the court

RULES OF THE GAME

The rules are designed to make squash safe and enjoyable

SQUASH IS A FAST AND EXCITING GAME, played in a confined area, so strict rules are vital to ensure safe and fair competition. Physical contact between players is inevitable during an intense contest as both struggle to secure positional advantage, but the rules prevent brute force from influencing the outcome. There are also regulations concerning the swing of your racket. However, the most important factors in making squash safe are consideration and common sense. These are especially important in social squash, because you will rarely have a referee. Both players must be prepared to exercise patience and restraint so that a vigorous and enjoyable match can take place without undue risk of injury.

• **RACKET**
An excessive follow-through could hit your opponent at head height.

SAFETY

During a game of squash, both players sprint around the court as they play their shots and also try to return to the T quickly. This means that inevitably, from time to time, they will get in one another's way. Close proximity also means that the racket, backswing, or follow-through of each shot could hit the other player. There is also a risk that players might be hit by the ball. These factors mean that safety is of prime importance. Each player must be aware of what his opponent is doing and where he is standing, in order to avoid contact.

ARM •
Use your free arm to keep you steady as you play your shot and prepare for the next one.

FOLLOW-THROUGH
An exaggerated follow-through is not only dangerous, it is illegal and could result in you losing the point if the referee judges that you were playing recklessly.

• **FEET**
Move your feet early to improve positioning and follow-through.

THE BASIC RULES OF SQUASH

SERVING

• A "coin toss" or "racket spin" is used to decide who serves first. The server chooses the box he is going to serve from, and proceeds to alternate between the two boxes until he loses the serve. The new server elects a box and also alternates until his opponent wins the serve back.

The server must ensure one foot is completely within the box

• A serve must reach above the **cut line** and land in the opposite back section of the court, although the ball can hit the side or back walls before it bounces. If it lands below the cut line or outside the opposite quarter, the serve is passed to the receiver.

• The server must have at least one foot inside the service box when serving. The serve must hit the front wall before any other wall – if the ball goes "out" above the front, side, or back wall, or goes into the **tin**, the other player gets to serve.

THE BALL

• After a serve, the ball may be played off any wall or walls, but it must always strike the front wall before it bounces on the floor.

• The ball may bounce only once on the floor. If a ball bounces twice or more, it is described as "down" or "not up", and directly loses the striker the **rally**.

A player must make every effort to reach the ball

• The racket can only make contact with the ball once on each shot. A "double" hit is illegal and loses the striker the rally.

AWARDING A LET

• If a player is prevented from reaching the ball or making a clean shot, he should stop play and ask for a **let**. If, however, he continues to play, or attempts to make a shot, no let is awarded.

• No let will be given if it is thought that the appealing player would not have reached the ball anyway, or if the player did not make a genuine effort to reach and play the ball. If a shot is attempted and missed, a let will not be awarded unless there was obvious **interference** on the opponent's backswing.

• If a let is awarded (or agreed to between the players when no referee is present), the **rally** is played again. A let will be awarded if a player would have got to the ball but was prevented from doing so by interference from his opponent.

AWARDING A STROKE

• If a **rally** is stopped when one opponent has played fairly and is in a clear, winning situation, a stroke is awarded. The player awarded the stroke wins the rally.

• A stroke is also awarded to the striker if **interference** occurs when he is in a clear, winning situation, or if his opponent fails to make a reasonable effort to get out of the way of the striker, ball, or racket.

• When the striker plays the ball and it hits his opponent, a stroke is awarded to the striker if it is clear that the ball would have hit the front wall first. If the ball would have hit the side wall first, a let is played. "Blind" strokes from the back corner that hit the opponent result in a **let**.

SCORING

• Games are played up to 9 points, with points being scored by the server only. At 8–8, the receiver may choose whether to play up to 9 points (known as "no set"), or up to 10 (known as "set two").

• Alternatively, games can be played up to 15 points, with both server and receiver being able to score throughout each **rally**. At 14–14, the receiver shall decide whether to play up to 15 or 16.

The ball may bounce, and make contact with the racket, only once

SHAPING UP

Strong muscles and stamina enable you to enjoy squash to the full

WHEN YOU PLAY SQUASH, you must be supple enough to reach for the ball; strong enough to generate powerful shots; and have enough stamina to see you through a whole match. The areas to concentrate on are your stomach, legs, and arms. A thorough warm-up before your game is crucial if you are to avoid feeling sore the next day.

OFF-COURT

Exercise off-court to get your muscles and heart strong enough for the games to come

Lock your • arms at the elbows and keep your fingers straight

FLEXIBILITY

Supple limbs are vital when playing squash. One second you are having to bend low to play your stroke, while the next you are having to reach up high. You will also find yourself sprinting around the court, starting, stopping, and changing your direction in quick succession – all of which is very demanding on your legs. Exercises that help to improve flexibility should form part of your fitness programme. Always jog on the spot for a minute or two before starting a game.

• *Move in a smooth curve to touch your toes*

TOUCH YOUR TOES
Stand with your legs about 2ft (60cm) apart. Hold your arms horizontally. With straight legs, alternate between touching your right toes with your left hand and your left toes with your right hand. Repeat 20 times.

• *Lift your leg onto a bench and straighten the knee as you lift up*

STEP-UPS
Step up and down on a bench or box, about 1ft (30cm) high, leading with your right foot for one minute, then with your left foot for another.

LEG-THRUST
Squat with your weight on your arms. Thrust your legs out behind you and then draw your knees back up to your chest. Repeat 20 times.

STRENGTH

It is useful to be able to hit with power and to have the endurance to keep going during a long match, so exercises that help to improve strength are essential. You should exercise for about one hour, two to three times a week to develop fitness and strength. Never neglect the warm-up exercises before going on-court, as these will ensure that the muscles you are strengthening in your overall fitness program are completely warmed up. Exercising will make you stronger and more flexible, but don't exercise in order to become a body-builder. Muscles are heavy and if you acquire muscle bulk, you will simply have more weight to carry around.

Lift with your • knuckles pointing at the ceiling, then turn them back

ARM PRESS
Holding a light weight in each hand, bring your arms up from your sides to a horizontal position. Try to complete three sets of ten lifts.

•Stand with your legs about 15cm (6in) apart for this exercise

• Hold your legs straight, with your weight on your toes

Keep your elbows • clear of your body

PUSH UPS
Lie on your stomach, keep your body rigid, and push yourself up using your arms. Try to complete three sets of ten push-ups each.

ROTATING SIT-UPS
Lie on your back with your knees bent. Sit up and alternate between touching your left knee with your right elbow and vice versa. Complete three sets of ten sit-ups.

• Touch, but don't lift with your hands

• Push your weight down to keep your partner's feet firmly on the floor

Twist at the • waist as you reach for your knee with your elbow

ON-COURT

Stretching your muscles on-court before starting to play is essential if you want to enjoy good squash and avoid the risk of injury and stiffness

TORSO

Squash involves much more than merely using your hands and arms to hit a ball with a racket. Most on-court movement requires stretching and twisting of your whole body, so it is crucial to warm up the large pads of muscle in your shoulders and neck, your stomach, and your back. If you play without loosening them first, you could tear the muscle fibers when you make a lunge for the ball. The pain from this sort of injury is not only agonizing, it can put you out of action for weeks. Apart from risking serious injury, muscles that are not warmed up enough before use will not work nearly as efficiently as those that are.

• *Rotate your head gently in both directions*

NECK STRETCH
Relax the muscles in your neck and upper back before a game by rotating your head halfway in a clock-wise direction, and then counter-clockwise.

Reach behind • *your head and cup your elbow in your hand*

ARM STRETCH
Pull one elbow behind your head and then the other, to stretch the back of your upper arm and shoulder, enabling you to swing more freely.

Keep the right side of • *your body on the floor as you lift your leg*

SIDE STRETCH
Lie on your back and extend your right arm to your right. Lift your right leg across your left one. Repeat ten times, and begin again, using opposite limbs.

• *Point your arm out flat and straight*

Hold your arms • *shoulder width apart*

• *Use your back muscles to lift yourself as high as possible*

BACK STRETCH
Lie on your stomach and lift your head, shoulders, arms, and legs into the air (only as far as is comfortable). Hold the position for two seconds and relax. Repeat ten times to warm your lower back muscles.

LEGS

In a game that involves as much running as squash does, strong leg muscles give you a great advantage. You need to be able to leap and stretch to reach fast and high balls. There are three main areas of the legs: the front and back of the thighs, and the back of the calves. After stretching and before vigorous exercise, it is a good idea to jog on the spot for a minute or two to loosen up your legs and body. Remember that you can't stretch your leg muscles too much.

CALF STRETCH
Lean against a wall and extend a leg behind you. Stretch the back leg by pressing down with your heel.

Push firmly against the wall for balance

• *Put your weight onto your bent leg to allow the other one to stretch*

• *Steady yourself by placing your hand against the wall*

FRONT OF THIGH
Balance with one hand against a wall and stand on the leg nearest the wall. Hold the ankle of your bent leg and pull it back. Swap sides and repeat with the other leg.

• *Feel the muscles stretching as you pull backward*

BACK OF THIGH
Adopt a half-squatting position, with one leg slightly bent and the other held straight. Move your hips back to stretch the back of the thigh of your straight leg. Swap legs and repeat the move.

Pull back on your heel •

Use your arm for balance •

SPRINTS
Sprint from one side of the court to the other. Touch the **nick** between the wall and floor at each turn.

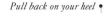

THE WEEKEND COURSE

Understanding the Weekend Course at a glance

THE COURSE COVERS nine skills in two days. The skills included on the first day refer to the basic forehand and backhand ground strokes, moving on to the other essential squash strokes – **volleys, drops**, and **lobs** – later in the day. The second day teaches you the more sophisticated shots such as **angle shots**. Strategic playing methods, such as how to keep your opponent on the defensive while you try to **kill** the **rally,** are also explained. After the first day, you will be able to play an enjoyable rally. At the end of the second day, you should be able to engage in a proper match.

DAY 1		Hours	Page
SKILL 1	Forehand ground stroke	1¹/₂	24
SKILL 2	Backhand ground stroke	1¹/₂	30
SKILL 3	Volleying	1	36
SKILL 4	The drop	1	44
SKILL 5	The lob	1	48

*Backswing for the high **volley** backhand (p.43)*

Being prepared for the perfect forehand stroke (p.28)

Solo practice routines, using the backhand (p.33)

KEY TO SYMBOLS

CLOCKS

A small clock marks the start of each new skill. The blue part is a guide to how much time you may need to spend learning that skill, and the grey segment shows where the skill fits into your day. The clock does not indicate the time it will take you to apply any particular maneuver, but how much time you might spend practicing each skill until you feel confident. Don't worry if you are taking longer than the designated times – they are just a guide.

RATING SYSTEM •••••

The complexity of a skill is rated by a bullet system based on a scale of one to five. One bullet (•) denotes that the skill is relatively easy to acquire, while five-bullet (•••••) skills are the most challenging.

ARTWORK ANALYSIS

The solid blue line (bl) and broken pink line (pl) used on the court diagrams show the flight of the ball: the (bl) is discussed in the accompanying caption, while the (pl) indicates a return or alternative shot.

Forehand angle shots from the front of the court (p.56)

Disguising the backswing for the forehand drop (p.44)

Using the walls and angles of the court to play across-court (p.53)

Hitting through the forehand lob (p.49)

Regular grip for forehand strokes (p.24)

1 FOREHAND GROUND STROKE

Definition: *Provides a range of shots, from power-**drives** to delicate strokes*

SQUASH IS A GAME OF POWER AND PRECISION. Of all the weapons in your armory, the basic forehand is the most important because it allows you to hit the ball, either hard or soft, with great accuracy. It is also a shot that comes quite naturally to the novice player. Even if you have never held a racket before, you can still make a promising attempt at hitting the ball using this stroke. However, you should never take the forehand for granted; it may seem straightforward, but it is crucial to get this stroke right from the moment you start learning to play. It will be one of the main foundations of your game, so don't be tempted to proceed without mastering this skill first.

OBJECTIVE: To gain the winning edge with a perfected forehand. *Rating •*

GETTING TO GRIPS

  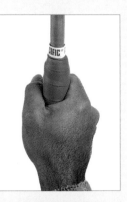

REGULAR GRIP	**"JAHANGIR" GRIP**	**INCORRECT GRIP**
Form a "V" between your thumb and forefinger over the top, inside edge of the racket handle. Allow your fingers to wrap around it to form a firm, secure grip.	Grip the racket further up the handle and turn it so that the top, inside edge of the handle moves to the right. This allows **slice** to be added to your forehand.	In the above example, the racket is turned too far to the inside. This will mean that the face is angled, causing you to hit the ball either too high or too low.

BASIC FOREHAND

*Preparation is the key to good squash. Make sure that
your grip feels secure, and get into position early*

RACKET
Keep control of
your racket –
from the top of
the backswing
to the end of the
follow-through.

KNEES
Keep your knees
bent. This will
make it much
easier, both to
move around
the court and to
inject more power
into your shots.

STANDING FIRM

As soon as you have played your shot,
get ready to play the next. **Rallies** are
lost when one player is caught out of
position and does not have time to get
ready for the next stroke. Always try
to recover both the T and the ideal
stance immediately after playing your
shot. Remember that you can reach
every part of the court from the T,
without having to struggle. You may
find it difficult to discipline yourself
in the early stages but, with practice,
it will become almost a reflex action.

FEET
Keep on the balls of your feet so that you can
recover the T quickly and get your body into
position ready to play the next shot. If you
are caught flat-footed, you will lose the rally.

PRACTICE ROUTINES

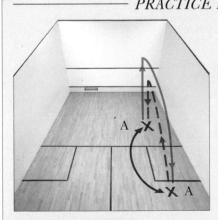

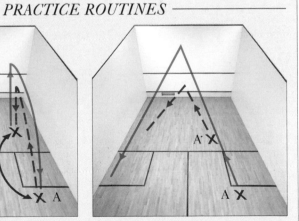

FOREHAND DRIVES
Practice forehand **drives** down the right-
hand wall. Start at the front of the court.
Play high toward the back (bl), then move
back and play the ball low to the front (pl).
Sprint back and forth to develop a routine.

PACE & ACCURACY
To practice across-court, bounce the ball
off the side wall or floor and hit it at just
below knee height. To reach the back of
the court, aim the ball high onto the front
wall (bl). Concentrate on your swing.

1 DEVELOP YOUR FOREHAND

*By adding power and precision to the basic forehand, you
create a strong foundation on which to build your game*

• ARM
Think "Racket
back, arm up"
and do both
in one smooth
movement. By
doing so, you
help to ensure
good form.

Step 1
THE BACKSWING

For a good backswing, prepare early
so that you don't have to rush your
shot. Bend your racket arm at the
elbow and raise it above shoulder
height. Hold your free arm straight
out, pointing toward the ball, and
make sure the racket is held high.
In order to adopt the correct position,
maintain a straight line between the
fingertips of your free hand and your
racket elbow. Place weight mainly on
your back foot during the backswing,
but keep your knees loosely bent.

• EYES
Watch the ball as you strike it
to ensure your timing is correct.
Concentrate on hitting the ball
in the center of your racket.

• KNEES
Keep your knees
bent. You are like a
spring preparing to
unleash its power.

• FEET
Put your weight
onto your right
foot. Use your left
foot for balance.

Step 2
THE STRIKE

Bring your racket through a smooth
curve toward the ball and "press" into
the shot as you hit it (see opposite
page). It is essential to be aware of
the moment when the racket meets
the ball, to enable you to play the
shot accurately. To help you stay
in control of your strike,
try to concentrate on
pressing the ball with
the racket. As you hit,
transfer your weight
onto your front foot.

• LEG
Use your left leg
as an anchor to
help keep you
steady as you
pivot freely into
the shot.

• RACKET
Sweep your
racket through
evenly and
with power.

Step 3
FOLLOW-THROUGH

Never presume that your shot is over just because you have hit the ball – the follow-through is crucial to the shot. Press the ball, imagining that it gets stuck to your racket as you hit it, so the only way to set it free is by pressing forward for about 1ft (30cm). Allow the racket to complete the second half of the swing, which will send the ball in the desired direction. When you get the hit and the follow-through correct, the ball will go where you want it to go. Your follow-through should finish with the racket head close to where it began, as if you had drawn a circle in the air, using the racket as a pencil.

• ARM
Keep your arm
loosely bent to
allow the racket
to sweep smoothly
through a full arc.

• KNEES
Knees should be bent
so that you finish the
shot as well-balanced
as when you started.

POISE
Be ready to recover the T immediately after playing your shot. Remember, the mark of the best player is not the single, perfectly played shot, but the succession of good ones.

PRACTICE ROUTINES

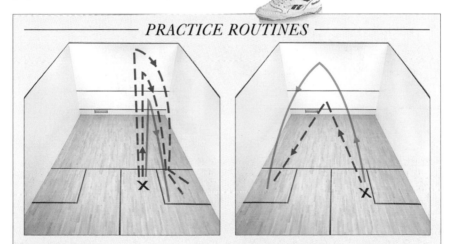

DOWN-THE-WALL
Play straight, landing the ball in the same area of the court with a low, hard shot (bl) as with a high soft one (pl). At first, just try to land shots in the service box. Reduce the size of your target as you improve.

ACROSS-COURT
Bounce the ball off the side wall or floor, or play a straight shot before hitting across-court. A controlled, softly struck ball that rebounds high off the front wall (bl) will go to the same spot as a low, hard **drive** (pl).

SKILL
1

PERFECT YOUR FOREHAND

Practice with a partner to develop speed, balance, and the necessary technique for a complete range of forehand strokes

Step 1

BE PREPARED

When you practice on your own, you are in complete control. When you add the other important ingredient – your opponent – you will be battling for control with another player. As you begin to hit the ball to each other, give yourself plenty of time to prepare for each shot. If you are out of position or struggling to reach the ball, you will lose control and give your opponent the opportunity to take the initiative.

EYES
Whether it is your shot or not, always keep an eye on the ball so that you are not caught out.

• RACKET
Remember the importance of the backswing – take the racket back high, in time for the shot.

• RACKET & BALL
The moment of contact between racket and ball is the most important in the **rally** – whether hitting or receiving.

Step 2

THE STRIKE

Whether practicing with a partner or playing in a match, concentrate fully on the power with which you hit the ball, and the direction in which you want it to go. It is not enough just to strike every ball as hard as you can. You have to maintain control so that you can place the ball with touch and precision. Remember to press (see p.27) the ball as you hit it – this enables you to utilize your racket head to maximum effect.

POSITION
If it is your partner's turn to strike, watch the ball and be prepared to move as soon as it leaves his racket.

---- Step 3 ----
FOLLOW-THROUGH

If you just stab at the ball, it is likely to travel slowly and in the wrong direction. Instead, use a flowing sweep to bring the racket head back almost to where it was at the beginning of the stroke, and the ball will travel directly to where you want it to go. Keep your wrist held firm to maintain control of the racket. Plant your feet wide apart to obtain a low center of gravity, and extend your free arm horizontally for stability. Push off from the front foot to recover the T.

FINISH HIGH
No matter how low the hit, the racket must always finish higher than your head. Never neglect the follow-through as it is fundamental to ensuring that your shots are accurate.

• **POSITIONING**
As soon as you have played your shot, return to the T, ready for the next one.

• **RACKET**
A high follow-through may feel exaggerated at first, but you will soon get used to it – and it has a winning effect on your shots.

PRACTICE ROUTINES

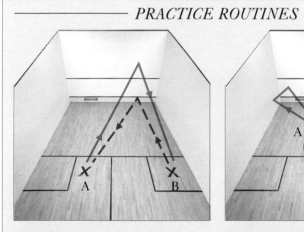

HITTING TO A LENGTH
With a partner, aim at different heights on the front wall. Vary the pace to achieve shots of consistent line and length. Player (A) must turn his back to the left-hand wall to play a forehand (bl) across-court to (B).

WORKING THE CORNERS
With a partner, use the corner angles at the front-of-court to bring the ball back to the center. After (A) has played to the left (bl), he moves to the T, while (B) moves from the T to play to the right-hand corner (pl).

SKILL

DAY 1

2 BACKHAND GROUND STROKE³

Definition: *Generates pace or delivers a delicate touch for a balanced game*

THE BACKHAND, UNLIKE THE FOREHAND, is not a stroke that comes naturally – it has to be learned. It is, however, just as crucial as the forehand, so add it to your repertoire as soon as possible. As it is not always possible to get into the forehand position in time to make a return shot, it is essential that you are able to play equally well on both sides of the court; in doing so, you will also be able to exploit its angles. For this reason, you must work on your backhand until it becomes as easy a stroke to play as the forehand. You will then be able to play a wider range of shots from every part of the court, and will be well on the way to a fully rounded game.

OBJECTIVE: To gain a thorough knowledge of the backhand. *Rating* ••

GETTING TO GRIPS

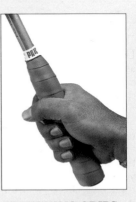

REGULAR GRIP
Hold the racket at the base of the shaft. This allows the full, unbroken arc of the swing to be made, which in turn creates greater power in your backhand stroke.

"JAHANGIR" GRIP
Hold the racket further up the handle. This makes the swing "shorter", but it also gives you more control over the racket head; this can be useful when playing a **rally**.

SWITCHING GRIPS
Most players use only one grip, but if you need to switch, hold the racket at the neck with your free hand while you reposition your racket hand.

BASIC BACKHAND

*An effective backhand is essential because **rallying** demands that you are able to play good strokes from both sides of your body*

PRACTICE ROUTINES

BACKHAND DRIVES
Hit low and hard from the back-of-court so that the ball bounces at the front (bl), then move to the front and play softly to the back (pl). Go back and forth between shots. Keep the ball close to the wall.

TIME & PERSEVERANCE
Bounce the ball off the side wall or floor to prepare to play across-court. Aim hard and low (bl) to develop accuracy and control. A controlled swing and follow-through will produce sufficient power.

READY FOR ACTION

During a **rally**, you will be unsure as to whether your next shot will be a forehand or a backhand, so it is wise to adopt a stance that enables you to play either. Stand steady with your weight evenly distributed. Hold the racket in front of you and make sure your grip is firm. Concentrate on the ball and be ready to move swiftly to your left or right. Think about the trajectory of the ball, move to meet it, and strike. Then, most importantly, recover your stance for the next shot.

CONCENTRATE
If the backhand feels a little uncomfortable when you first try it, concentrate on hitting the ball in the middle of the racket. This also helps you to improve your timing.

RACKET •
Hold the racket in front of you at a 45° angle. If you hold it any closer, you restrict your body movement; lower, and it will be harder to make the backswing.

KNEES •
Keep your knees bent so that they are ready to propel you quickly to your next position.

SKILL

DEVELOP YOUR BACKHAND

*Injecting power and accuracy into the backhand helps you to
rally effectively and, as you improve, to play attacking shots*

Step 1

THE BACKSWING

As with the forehand, the backswing
is a vital part of the backhand stroke.
Your shoulders play an important part
as you prepare to hit the ball. Turn
away from the ball, with the elbow of
your playing arm pointing down, and
the racket held almost vertically. You
will find that you are looking back
over your shoulder for the ball. Keep
your free arm clear of your body to
allow a full, smooth stroke and to
improve your balance. There should
be a smooth transfer of weight from
the back foot to the front foot to add
extra momentum to your shot.

SHOULDER
"Give" your shoulder
to the shot. The more
you swivel your body,
the more power you
give to the hit.

KNEES
Bend your knees to
absorb the transfer of
weight from one foot
to the other. Keep
your feet fairly close
together or you will
lose your balance.

HEAD
Keep your head down. If
you lift your head, you will
hit the ball too high. Look
at the ball, not at the target.

Step 2

THE STRIKE

RACKET
Try to hit the ball
away from your
body, in line with
your right foot.

FEET
Plant your feet about
shoulder width apart to
allow your body to turn.

Many beginners make the mistake of
just slashing at the ball in an attempt to
generate power. Consider power later.
At this stage it is far more important to
concentrate on simply hitting the ball
smoothly. The point of impact should
be about 1ft (30cm) in front of your
right leg and about the same distance
from the floor. Press (see p.27) the
ball as you strike it; this will help
you to keep control of the racket
head in order to send the ball in the
chosen direction. If your swing feels
jerky or awkward, give yourself a little
more time to prepare for the shot.

Step 3
FOLLOW-THROUGH

Control is crucial when you play the backhand, because if you take a wild swipe at the ball, there is a danger that you could hit your partner on the follow-through. To maintain control, press the ball for at least 1ft (30cm) to give it direction and to keep your follow-through compact. You will also find that if you keep your arm relaxed rather than rigid, the racket will travel across your body to finish high and pointing up at the ceiling, as opposed to flat and waving dangerously into the open-court. Keep your eyes on the ball and your head still. Once your stroke is completed, return to the T in preparation for your next shot.

• RACKET
After you have played the stroke, your racket should be almost vertical. Quickly bring it back down in front of you.

ARM •
Keep your arm gently bent at the elbow. If it is stiff, you will be unable to complete a smooth swing.

LEGS •
Your legs should act as stabilizers until you have made your shot. All the weight is now on your front foot and you are ready to push off for your next shot.

CONTROL
Concentrate on a full, smooth follow-through. This helps you to control the shot so that it goes where you want it to go. It also brings you back to a more upright position, from which you can recover the T quickly.

PRACTICE ROUTINES

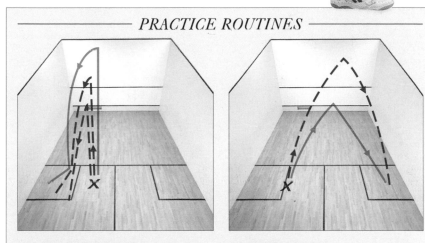

PLAYING STRAIGHT
Hit the ball to various heights on the front wall, but practice reaching a consistent length by aiming to bounce the ball on the **short line**. Pay extra attention to the high shot (bl), which demands more control.

ACROSS-COURT
Bounce the ball or play a straight **drive** to set up high (pl) and low (bl) backhand shots across the court. When you can hit the ball hard enough, a shot aimed just above the **tin** will bounce **deep** into the back-of-court.

PERFECT YOUR BACKHAND

Practice with a partner to develop speed, balance, and technique, for a complete range of backhand shots

RACKET •
Your racket has to travel far before it hits the ball, so time your swing correctly.

Step 1
PREPARATION

The backhand is not as natural a shot to play as the forehand, so it is most important that you allow plenty of time to prepare for it. Turn the shoulder of your racket arm toward the front wall, bend your arm at the elbow, and hold your racket up high. From this position, you are able to generate maximum power. Consider where you need to stand in order to produce a full, smooth swing and a clean contact with the ball.

STANCE
Twist your body as much as you can so that you are able to swing the racket with speed and so give power to your shot.

Step 2
THE STRIKE

It is more important to control your racket than to generate power. Hold the racket firmly in front of you as you make contact with the ball. Your arm should now be slightly bent and your wrist supple enough to whip the racket through the hit. Once you are confident that your timing is correct, start increasing the speed of your strokes until you are striking the ball with great power.

CONTROL
Keep the swing as smooth and controlled as possible. Erratic movements will adversely affect the pace and direction of the shot.

• EYES
You will only connect correctly with the ball by keeping your eyes fixed on the path of its flight.

Step 3
FOLLOW-THROUGH

Completing the follow-through on the backhand is vital if you are to perfect the stroke. Pull out of the backswing too soon and you will lose power and accuracy – try it and see. To bring the racket smoothly through the stroke, turn your shoulders so that your body swivels toward the front of the court. Swing your racket arm as far behind you as it will go; this will allow your racket to finish high. Hold your wrist firm so that you remain in command of the racket head, which should be higher than your shoulder. Control the follow-through so that your racket does not lash out at your partner.

• RACKET
The racket head should finish high and point upward. Once the stroke is complete, prepare yourself for the next one.

MOBILITY
It is important to keep some bounce in your knees at all times so that you are ready to return quickly to the T in preparation for the next shot.

PRACTICE ROUTINES

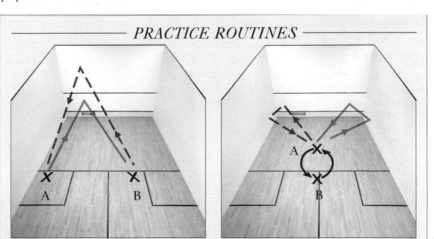

HITTING TO A LENGTH
With a partner, hit across-court. Player (A) should hit low and hard (bl), while player (B) should hit high and soft (pl). Player (B), on the right-hand side of the court, should have his back to the right-hand wall.

WORKING THE CORNERS
Use the front corners to bring the ball back to the center. Player (A) should hit to the right-hand corner (bl) then move to the T, while player (B) should move forward and play to the left (pl). Develop a routine.

3 VOLLEYING

Definition: *Striking the ball before it bounces on the floor*

THE ABILITY TO HIT THE BALL before it bounces on the floor is crucial to playing good squash. **Volleying** – taking the ball "on the fly" – is necessary, for example, when you are on the T and want to intercept your opponent's **drive** toward the back of the court. The volley shot allows you to play the ball early and thus seize the initiative. You can also use this stroke to attack, or to gain time in which to improve your defense. The earlier you play the ball, the more difficult the shot becomes for your opponent, so get into position quickly. When you first practice volleying, you may find yourself swiping at thin air, but persevere: an effective volley will enable you to develop well beyond the basic level.

OBJECTIVE: To play the ball at the earliest opportunity. *Rating ••••*

FOREHAND VOLLEY

This shot can be powerful or delicate. In either case, it is vital to keep a smooth racket action

• **RACKET**
Keep your racket head held high so that even with a short backswing you can whip up sufficient power for the **volley**.

—————— Step 1 ——————
THE BACKSWING

The preparation for the **volley** backswing is similar to that for a forehand **drive**, but because the volley is played before the ball bounces, you will not have time to take the racket back so far. To compensate, generate power by straightening your racket arm at the elbow as you strike, and direct the shot by using a **flick** of your wrist. The ball will be higher for a volley, so you may need to adjust your swing, but ensure you follow-through properly.

• **LEGS**
Plant legs apart to gain a lower center of gravity. Keep some bounce in your knees so you are ready to sprint.

• **FEET**
As you prepare to hit, move your weight from your back foot to your front foot. Stay on the balls of your feet.

Steps 2 & 3
HITTING THROUGH

A well-played **volley** is a "meaty" shot
that uses the full spring of your racket
strings. Concentrate on striking the
ball in the center of the racket to
gain power and control. Remember
to press it as you make contact. Allow
your weight to move forward as you
hit the ball, to give extra impetus to
the shot – essential because of the
shortened backswing. By playing
the volley shot, you will have
speeded up the **rally**, so quickly
recover your position on the T.

ARM
Point your arm at
the left-wall **nick**.
This opens up the
front of your body
and so allows a full,
smooth swing.

STRIKE
Take the ball
slightly in front
of you and press
it on contact.
Use a **flick** of
your wrist to
give it direction.

EYES
To preserve
your balance,
focus on the
point where
your racket
hits the ball.

FOREHAND

FINISHING
As you follow through,
keep the racket head
flat so that it finishes
in front of – not over –
your left shoulder.

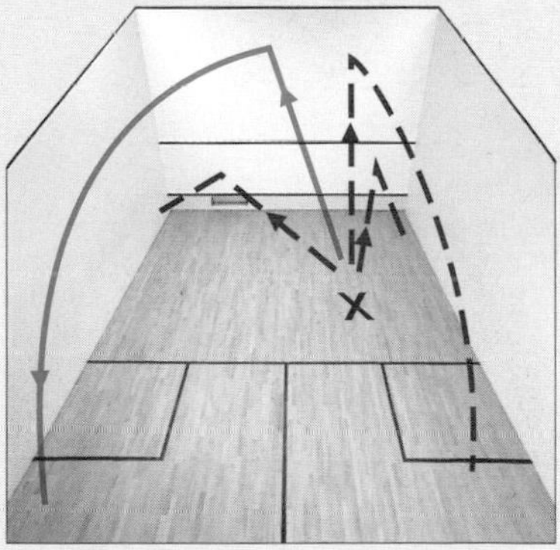

Practice hitting forehand **volleys** to
various parts of the court at different
speeds. In a match, a cross-court shot
to the back corner (bl) will force your
opponent out of position and give you
time to recover the T. Aiming low on
the front wall (pl) can win you the **rally**.

3

BACKHAND VOLLEY

To be confident on both sides of the court, learn to play the backhand **volley** *as smoothly and efficiently as the forehand*

───── Steps 1 & 2 ─────

PREPARE AND STRIKE

The backhand **volley** requires great flexibility in the upper body. Swivel at the waist and turn so that your right shoulder faces the front wall. Draw the racket back high, rather than have it pointing along your spine to the floor, and keep your right elbow up and away from your chest. Put your weight onto the your foot and use your right to balance. Position yourself so that you have room to swing your arm and racket in one smooth curve. Bring your weight forward onto both feet as you play the shot. Use your free arm to help you maintain balance.

BACKSWING
Hold your racket and elbow high and away from your chest so that your shoulder almost touches your chin.

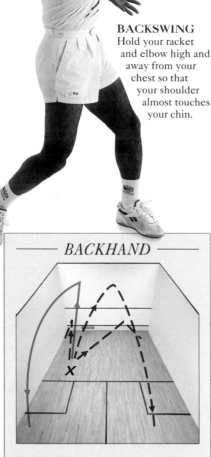

• ARM
Hold your arm straight as you strike the ball. Your wrist must be held firm to keep control.

─── *BACKHAND* ───

The down-the-wall **volley** is a useful **rally** shot. It is most effective if the ball "clings" to the wall all the way to the back corner (bl) . This makes it hard for your opponent to intercept, and adds to the difficulties of playing an attacking, return shot from the back of the court.

• FEET
Start with most of your weight on your left foot.

THE HIT
Watch the ball as it hits your strings, and press it as you return the shot. Hold your wrist and elbow in a straight line, parallel to the floor.

Step 3
FOLLOW-THROUGH

Perform a full follow-through as you spread your weight evenly between both feet. This smooth movement brings you round to face the front of the court so that you are ready to continue the **rally**. Don't cut your follow-through short in the hope that you will have more time to prepare for the next shot – this will only prevent you from controlling your **volley**. Although it is important to anticipate what might happen next in the rally, it is vital that you play each shot properly.

• **EYES**
Track the ball onto the wall. This enables you to prepare early for your opponent's return shot.

• **ARM**
Use your free arm to maintain balance while your racket arm is completing the follow-through.

• **RACKET**
The racket will finish behind you. Bring it back in front of you, ready for the next shot.

FEET •
Keep on the balls of your feet so that you are ready to spring back quickly to the T.

TIMING THE STRIKE

TRACKING THE BALL
The point where the ball bounces on the floor helps you to determine where it is in relation to you. Without the bounce, the judgement is more difficult to make. For the **volley**, therefore, you need to gauge the flight and speed of the ball as it leaves the front wall, and then calculate the exact moment to make your strike.

FEELING THE IMPACT
Make contact when the ball is 6in (15cm) in front of your body. Press (see p.27) through the ball and try to feel its weight on your strings. This fleeting moment is your last chance to influence the direction and speed of the ball. The more you focus on the hit, the more control you have, but don't interrupt the swing when you hit – keep a flowing movement, with the impact simply being a point along the full curve.

• *Hit in the center of your racket for power and control*

• *Keep your eyes on the ball as you hit*

• *Use your free arm to help keep you stable while you stretch*

• *Keep some bounce in your legs so that you can react quickly*

THE LOW VOLLEY

Volleys hit hard and low make a powerful attack and so are an effective way to win a rally

RACKET •
The short backswing makes it vital to press (see p.27) the ball and track it onto the strings.

—————— Steps 1 & 2 ——————
FOREHAND ATTACK

Any squash player will greatly enjoy hammering the ball low into the front wall so that it rebounds into the **nick** between the side wall and the floor. If you get the shot right, it is likely to be impossible for your opponent to make a return, but even if he does, he will be in a poor position to retrieve the next shot. To seize the initiative, play this shot at waist level, from the front of the court. If the ball is lower than your waist, reach for the early **volley** to rob your opponent of recovery time.

BACKSWING
Hit the ball slightly in front of you, using a short backswing. If you strike later, you will not inject enough power and you could also lose your balance.

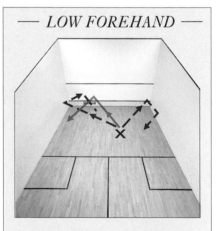

— *LOW FOREHAND* —

Practice low forehand **volleys** into both of the front corners. Try to make the ball hit the front wall and then "die" in the **nick** (bl). Even if the ball just misses the nick, it is likely to bounce awkwardly and so be difficult for your opponent to return.

ARM •
Point out your free arm for stability. Imagine a straight line from one hand to the other.

• **LEG**
Keep your center of gravity low by extending your left leg behind you.

LOW VOLLEY
Bend your right knee to get low. Since most of the power comes from a **flick**, keep your wrist loose. You must get the racket face right underneath the ball.

Steps 1 & 2
BACKHAND ATTACK

Use the backhand **volley** shot to
intercept a loose, cross-court **drive** or
a short, down-the-wall shot. It may
seem a difficult shot to master but, as
it can win you many **rallies**, it is well
worth persevering with it. Take the
ball as early as you can to enable you
to maximize your backswing and to
stay well balanced. Keep pressure on
your opponent by playing a **short ball**
into the corners, using the low backhand volley. Volleying gives your
opponent less
time to prepare.

LOW BACKHAND

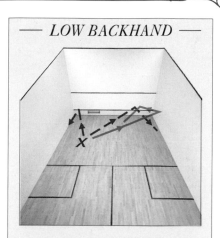

One option is the **reverse angle**, where
you play across the court onto the side
wall first (bl). This is a difficult shot, but
it can be very effective. The nearer the
ball is to the front wall when it hits the
side wall, the more difficult it will be for
your opponent to return.

• RACKET
Bring the bottom edge
of the racket through
first to "cut" the ball low
into the wall, making it
drop sharply into court.

WAIST HIGH
Hold your wrist firm to
press the ball home. Keep
your forearm parallel to the
front wall. Use the pace of
the ball off the strings to
give power to your shot.

LEGS •
Keep your legs apart
for extra stability.
Put your weight
onto your left foot.

• EYES
Watch the ball
as it hits the
strings – in the
very center of
your racket.

• WRIST
Hold your wrist firm,
but keep it supple
enough to allow a
flick if desired.

LOW VOLLEY
Keep a low center of gravity by putting your
right leg forward and your left leg well behind
you. Get into position quickly so that you can
concentrate on playing the shot itself.

THE HIGH VOLLEY

*The high **volley** is the best shot to prevent a loose serve,
lob, or high **drive** from reaching the back of the court*

Steps 1 & 2
FOREHAND

As with all **volleys**, there is no bounce
to help you gauge the trajectory of
the ball, so concentration is vital.
Think of the forearm action as
similar to an overarm throw, but
remember to keep control of the
racket head. Use your free arm as a
gun-sight to track the ball. The racket
face is only at the top of its path for a
moment, so precise timing is crucial.
Hit the ball slightly in front as your
racket travels downward. This
will angle it onto the front wall.

• ARM
As you reach for the
ball, stretch your free
arm up high to help
you track the ball and
maintain balance.

PREPARATION
Point at the ball
with your free hand,
keeping your arm
straight. Hold the
racket vertical and
your racket arm
bent at the elbow.
Put your weight
onto the right foot.

• ARM
Whip through with
your wrist, elbow,
and shoulder,
but ensure the
hit is accurate
and controlled.

FEET •
Launch yourself into the
shot by pushing upward
from the balls of your feet.
Don't be caught flat-footed.

THE HIT
"Throw" the racket
head at the ball to
make a powerful
shot. To add extra
momentum, turn
to face the front of
the court as you hit
the ball. Transfer
all of your weight
onto your left foot.

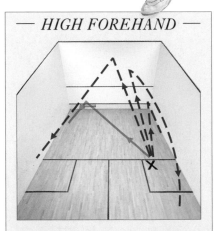

— HIGH FOREHAND —

When in the middle of the court, **kill**
the high **volley** by angling it off the
front wall so that it lands in the **nick**
between the left-hand side wall and the
floor (bl). When you are at the back of
the court, play the ball down-the-wall or
across-court to the opposite back corner.

RACKET
Hold your racket so that its head is parallel to the floor behind your head, not pointing up at the ceiling.

LEG
Use your back leg to push you toward the ball and to provide extra balance.

BACKSWING
Keep your racket face flat to maximize your backswing, and watch the ball closely over your right shoulder. Put your weight onto your back foot.

Steps 1 & 2
BACKHAND

The backhand high **volley** can be an awkward shot to play, because you have to turn away from the front wall in order to prepare for the hit. This can make it more difficult for you to recover for the next shot. It is also harder to control the racket during the high, backhand swing, so concentrate on a smooth action, using your shoulder, elbow, and wrist. The high volley requires timing, balance, and accuracy but, once mastered, it will add winning skills to your game by allowing you to use attacking shots that prevent balls from reaching the back of the court.

WRIST
A firm wrist keeps the racket steady. A final "snap" as you hit the ball gives it extra punch and direction.

UPPER BODY
Use your upper body to reach and turn. Your arm cannot work in isolation, so move your body in one flowing movement.

THE HIT
To generate power, straighten out your racket arm from your elbow. Hold your wrist firm, but keep it flexible enough to allow you to angle the ball downward. For added power, transfer your weight onto your front foot as you strike the ball.

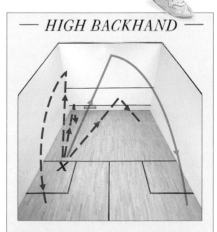

— HIGH BACKHAND —

The high backhand **volley** can **kill** the **rally** or place the ball out of reach. For example, the cross-court shot to the opposite back corner (bl) is useful when your opponent is at the front-of-court. Aim just below the front wall **out line**. Alternatively, play down-the-wall (pl).

4 THE DROP

Definition: *A ball played near the tin or along the side wall*

YOU CAN PLAY THE DROP from anywhere on the court to catch your opponent out of position. If the shot is played straight, the ball will cling to the side wall. Played across-court, it will land near the **nick** on either the first or second bounce, making it difficult to return. The **drop** is often an outright winner, but even if your opponent manages a return, there is a good chance that it will set up a winning opportunity for you. However, the drop can produce unforced errors if you hit the ball too low. Give yourself a margin for error and try to hit closer to the **tin** as you improve. Do not over-use the drop, or your opponent will begin to anticipate your intentions.

OBJECTIVE: To play an effective **drop** that will force your opponent out of position. *Rating* •••••

RACKET
By holding your racket up high, you can fool your opponent into expecting a strong **drive**.

FOREHAND DROP

*Disguise is important. If your opponent sees you are going to **drop**, the shot loses its effect*

— Step 1 —
THE BACKSWING

ARM
Straighten out your left arm to provide stability. Keep your knees bent to allow a smooth action.

FEET
Place weight onto your back foot as you prepare for the shot. Use your body to push into the ball.

Prepare for the **drop** as if you were going to **drive** the ball, by keeping your racket high. Your opponent will be unsure which shot you are about to play and will remain on the T. If you make it obvious that you are going to play the drop, your opponent will move to play the **short ball**. Balance is crucial because you need to control the strength of your swing so that you don't hit the ball hard. Plant your left foot forward and make a solid foundation with your right foot. Make sure your stance is correct, since a drop from an unstable position is unlikely to succeed. This shot calls for accuracy and control.

THE HIT

Last-second adjustments to the wrist can alter the direction of the **drop** and send your opponent in the wrong direction.

HITTING THROUGH

Use the hit and follow-through to determine the pace and direction of your **drop**. Take the ball as late as you can to aid your **disguise**, but allow time to get your racket underneath it. If you strike at the ball from above, it will be harder to control and easier to put into the **tin**. Force the bottom edge of the racket through first to add **slice** to the ball. This will bring it down sharply off the front wall. Use your wrist if you want to change the direction of the shot at the last minute. Keep the follow-through compact. This will help you to play a firm stroke without hitting it too hard or too high. After playing your shot, you may find yourself between your opponent and the ball – make every effort to give your opponent a chance to reach the ball.

• **RACKET**
Bring the bottom edge of the racket through first.

• **ARM**
Use your free arm to keep you steady as you follow through.

— FOREHAND DROP —

Practice straight **drops** from the front- and back-of-court. After playing a long drop from the back (pl), move forward to play a short drop at the front (bl). Angle the ball off the front wall so that it lands in the **nick**. The ball may miss the nick, but should still bounce near it.

COMPLETION
Keep your eyes on the ball to ensure that you raise your head which, in turn, will help you to balance and achieve a smooth follow-through.

BACKHAND DROP

SKILL
4

*Use the backhand to disguise **drops** played
either straight or across the court*

• RACKET
To prepare
for the hit,
point your
racket up at
the ceiling.

--- Steps 1 & 2 ---

PREPARE & STRIKE

Keep the racket high so that your
opponent cannot be sure which shot
you are going to play. Plant your right
foot toward the pitch of the ball and
concentrate on balance. The stroke
should be firm but controlled to
deliver sufficient, but not excessive,
power. Take the ball in front of you
and get the racket underneath to lift
it above the **tin**. Use a **flick** of your
wrist to change the angle of the racket
and so the direction of your shot. The
later you change this angle, the more
chance you have of deceiving your
opponent. Allow a margin for error
by aiming your shot well above the
tin. You will be able to hit lower as
you improve. Use the shot sparingly
or you will become predictable.

PREPARATION
Start with a high back-
swing and watch the
ball over your right
shoulder. Swivel from
the waist to turn your
back to the front wall.

• LEGS
Keep your legs
firm as you turn
the top half of
your body into
the shot.

THE STRIKE
Control the swing
to bring the racket
smoothly under the
ball. To ensure that
the ball drops, add
backspin to it by
slicing under it.

RACKET •
At the moment
of impact, push
the ball in the
right direction.

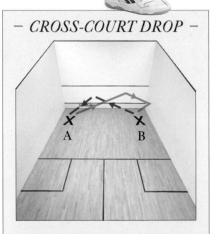

– *CROSS-COURT DROP* –

With a partner, practice playing across-
court toward the **nick**. If (A)'s shot hits
the side wall too high, it will be easy for
(B) to play, so work out the direction
and pace you need to use to achieve the
"dead roll" from the nick. Aim the ball
just above the **tin** to allow for mistakes.

Step 3
FOLLOW-THROUGH

The follow-through must be compact as you press (see p.27) or punch the ball onto the front wall, but it is also vital that your stroke is sufficiently well-defined to give the ball pace and direction. Watch the ball as it leaves your racket and track it onto the wall. This helps you to stay balanced and ensures you are quick to return to the T. Keep plenty of bounce in your legs so that you are ready to push off once you have completed the stroke. Don't just assume that your **drop** will be an instant winner and simply stand there expectantly. It is better to be ready for a shot that never comes than to lose the **rally** because of poor preparation.

SHOULDERS • Turn your shoulders smoothly as you complete the strike.

• LEGS Reach low for the ball by bending down at the hip and knee.

FOREHAND DROP VOLLEY

When you **volley**, you put your opponent into difficulties because you take the ball early. If you can play an attacking shot like the **drop** volley, you will have an excellent opportunity to win the **rally**. To play the drop volley, move into position quickly and stay well-balanced. Take the pace off the ball by absorbing its power with your racket. Keep your wrist and arm firm, and apply a little punch as you hit the ball, to give it the necessary weight and direction – it is no good just sticking your racket in

the way and hoping the ball bounces onto the front wall. Aim high to provide a margin of error above the **tin**. As you improve, your shots will hit nearer to the tin. The bottom of the racket should go through first to deliver "backspin", which will bring the ball down sharply and make it harder for your opponent to retrieve.

Hold your arm • straight out

• Bring the bottom edge of the racket through first to add "spin"

Keep your legs • apart for balance

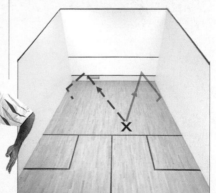

SHARP DROP
Backspin makes the ball travel sharply to the floor. Aim for the **nick**, whether playing to right (bl) or left. **Slice** under the ball as you hit to achieve this effect.

SKILL

DAY 1

5 THE LOB

Definition: *A ball played high over your opponent's head*

THE LOB IS A GREAT WAY to ease pressure and gain the initiative during a fast and furious **rally**. You can play the shot from the front or back of the court. Either way, it should force your opponent into a back corner and allow you to recover your ideal position. It is a shot that relies more on touch and precision than on power. Indeed, if you strike the ball too hard, it will either stray beyond the **out line** or bounce off the back wall into an inviting position for a **drive** or **kill** shot. On the other hand, if you hit the ball too low, it will set up your opponent nicely for a **volley** interception. However, when the **lob** is hit correctly, it can swiftly turn your defense into attack.

OBJECTIVE: To gain breathing space during the **rally**. *Rating* ••••

THE FOREHAND LOB

Played from the front of the court in the same position as the **drop***, this shot changes the pace of the* **rally**

Step 1

BACKSWING

The preparation for the **lob** can look like that used for the **drive** or **drop** shot. As a result, your intentions can be disguised to keep your opponent guessing about which shot you are about to play. Plant your left foot so that it points toward where the ball will bounce. Turn your left shoulder so that you are almost facing your side wall. This enables you to turn into the shot as you play it and to use your right foot for balance. Keep some bounce in your knees to allow you to bend easily. Your racket can start out high, but get the racket face well under the ball at the moment of impact. As the stroke begins, open the racket face by turning your wrist until the racket head is almost horizontal to the floor.

• **RACKET**
Start high, but quickly open the racket face so that you can lift the ball from underneath. Try to keep your wrist flexible, but firm.

LEGS •
Place your weight onto your left foot and use your right foot to help you balance.

Steps 2 & 3
HITTING THROUGH

In order to strike the ball to the back of the court without leaving yourself open to the **volley** interception, you will have to lift it over your opponent's head. To do this, get the face of the racket well under the ball and aim the shot about 18in (45cm) below the **out line** on the front wall. This provides height, without your having to use excessive power. The result, hopefully, will be that the ball drops gently into the back-of-court, where it is far more difficult for your opponent to make a return. If the ball rolls out of the **nick**, it will be impossible for him to return. A full follow-through helps the ball on its long journey.

• **RACKET**
Open the racket face by turning your wrist. Press the ball on impact.

THE HIT
This is not a powerful shot, but you must play it firmly in order for it to reach the back corner.

• **EYES**
Keep your eyes on the ball as it climbs the wall.

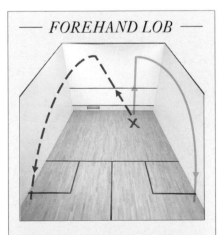

— *FOREHAND LOB* —

Play the **lob** down-the-wall to the back corner (bl) of the court. Aim 2ft (60cm) below the **out line** on the front wall to get enough height to prevent a **volley** interception. The cross-court version of the lob (pl), if played accurately, should reach the opposite back corner.

FINISHING
Sweep upward to add height and direction to your shot. The racket should finish high, and over your left shoulder.

SKILL

5

THE BACKHAND LOB

*It is vital that you have the ability to defend by using the
backhand stroke to play **lobs** to both back corners*

Steps 1 & 2

BACKSWING & HIT

• **EYES**
Track the ball to
a point in front
of you where it is
just high enough
to scoop upward.

BACKSWING
You can exaggerate the
backswing to deceive
your opponent, but for
the shot itself, you only
need to use a short,
smooth movement.

• **LEGS**
Even when your legs are
at full stretch, keep your
momentum going forward
to allow a full swing.

Use your body to help **disguise** your
intended shot, and keep your racket
held fairly high so that your opponent
cannot be sure whether you will play
short, **drive**, or **float** the **lob**. Move
your weight onto your right foot and
keep your feet well apart so that your
center of gravity is near the floor. Your
wrist should be held firm, but keep it
flexible enough to allow you to open
up the racket face on contact. Altering
the position of your wrist – using a
flick – can change the direction of the
ball right at the very last second, so
enabling you to vary between using a
down-the-wall, or cross-court lob. Hit
underneath the ball so that you can
lift it to a point high on the front wall,
about 18in (45cm) below the **out line**.

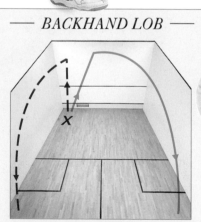

BACKHAND LOB

X

The cross-court option (bl) may feel
more natural on the backhand than the
down-the-wall shot (pl), as it allows a full
follow-through. Aim about 2ft (60cm)
below the **out line**. Hit various points on
the front wall to see how the trajectory
of the ball changes. Aim for the corner.

THE HIT
Bend at the knee and
waist to get low, and
play the ball when it
is in front of you so
that you have room
to sweep under it.

• **WRIST**
A **flick** of the wrist
provides an extra
push to the shot.

RACKET •
Get the racket underneath the
ball to lift the **lob** up high and
over the head of your opponent.

Step 3
FOLLOW-THROUGH

Effect a smooth and graceful follow-through as befits a shot that should soar high out of your opponent's reach to land safely in the back corner. So long as you have given the ball enough pace, it should reach the back of the court without hitting the ceiling or going out-of-court. Watch the ball as it strikes the front wall -- you will have to crane your neck, but this is a useful discipline that helps to ensure your follow-through is sufficient to launch the ball on the correct trajectory and at the right speed. Push off in plenty of time to prepare for any return shot your opponent might be able to make.

BACKSWING
You may choose to exaggerate the backswing to deceive your opponent, but for the shot itself, you only need a short, smooth stroke.

• RACKET
Bring the racket through high on the follow-through to ensure that the correct trajectory is given to the ball.

HIP •
Bend at your hip and knee to help lower your center of gravity. Be ready to push off quickly with your right leg.

FOOT •
Use your right foot as an anchor, but be ready to recover the T as soon as you have finished the shot.

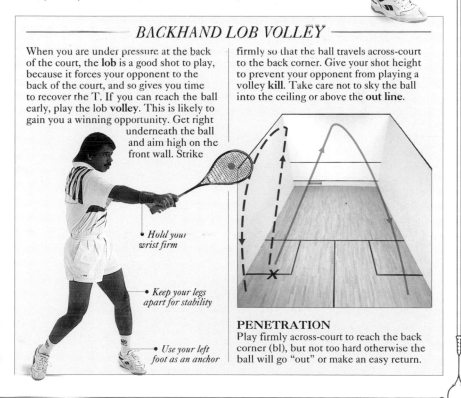

BACKHAND LOB VOLLEY

When you are under pressure at the back of the court, the **lob** is a good shot to play, because it forces your opponent to the back of the court, and so gives you time to recover the T. If you can reach the ball early, play the lob **volley**. This is likely to gain you a winning opportunity. Get right underneath the ball and aim high on the front wall. Strike firmly so that the ball travels across-court to the back corner. Give your shot height to prevent your opponent from playing a volley **kill**. Take care not to sky the ball into the ceiling or above the **out line**.

• Hold your wrist firm

• Keep your legs apart for stability

• Use your left foot as an anchor

PENETRATION
Play firmly across-court to reach the back corner (bl), but not too hard otherwise the ball will go "out" or make an easy return.

SKILL

6 WALL SHOTS

Definition: *Shots that use the walls to outwit your opponent*

SQUASH IS A GAME OF ANGLES. An experienced player uses the side and back walls to direct the ball where it is hardest to return, or to provide a route to the front wall that makes their opponent struggle. Watch what happens if you play a ball at certain speeds so that it rebounds at certain points. Fast balls behave differently than slow balls, and spin makes a real difference. If the ball goes into the corner, it can rebound twice. Once you are comfortable with executing rebounds, you will improve in both attack and defense.

OBJECTIVE: To introduce **angle shots** into your game. *Rating* ••••

REBOUNDS

*When the straight **drive** might be intercepted by a **volley** shot, use the walls to help the ball reach **deep** into the back of the court*

ACROSS-COURT

It can be hard to reach the back with a cross-court shot if your opponent is on the T. Using the side wall allows you to play wide and high so that the **volley** is no longer a threat. Aim for the corner, where the ball will be difficult to retrieve. Avoid rebounds that bring the ball into the middle of the court.

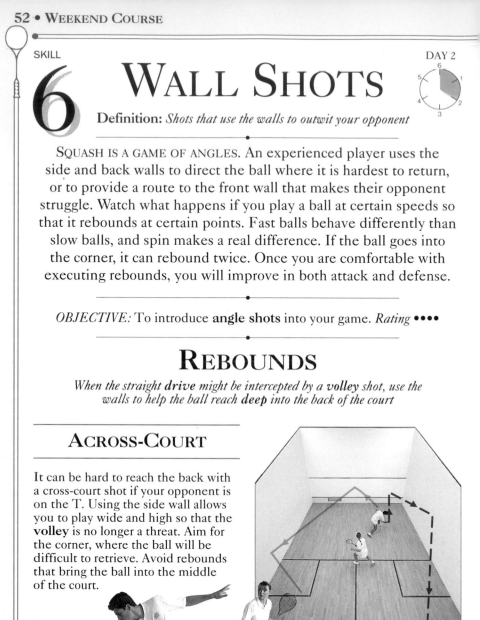

Open up your shoulders to allow the swing

AIM FOR THE CENTER
Aim toward the center of the front wall when playing across-court to the back of the court (bl). The further to the left you hit, the shallower the angle will be. This will cause the ball to rebound off the left-hand wall into court earlier than desired, and make it easier for your opponent to return.

BACK WALL & CORNER

If you play onto the front wall at an acute angle, use the **lob** or play high down-the-wall. If the ball strikes the back wall first, and then the side wall, it can be extremely difficult for your opponent to retrieve. Similarly, if it hits the back wall close to the floor, it can be impossible to return at all. The tighter into the corner you can make the ball land, the better. Remember, you will be punished for playing loose shots that bounce into the open-court.

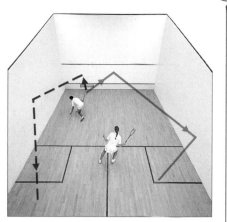

WIDTH & HEIGHT
It is essential to avoid giving your opponent the chance to **volley** your cross-court shot (bl). Width and height are the two means of reaching the back of the court without interception. If you hit high, use less power to stop the ball going "out", or bouncing off the side or back walls into an easy position.

DOWN-THE-WALL
When you play down-the-wall, angle your shot slightly so that it clings to the side wall (bl). This makes the shot extremely difficult for your opponent to defend. The ideal shot lands in the **nick** between the back wall and the floor. Non-nick balls should bounce on the floor rather than against the back wall.

—— USE ANGLES TO OUTFOX YOUR OPPONENT ——

THE THINKING GAME
A game of squash is not always won by the player who simply hits the hardest. Brains are just as important as brawn. Think about where your opponent is positioned, and use the angles to hit the ball to where it will be most difficult for him to return. Use touch and accuracy, as well as power.

DOMINATE THE COURT
The **boast** shot can catch your opponent out of position, especially if you disguise the shot to look like a straight **drive** or cross-court shot. Use the time it takes your opponent to return the ball to recover the T. Even if your opponent does manage to make a return, it is likely to be a poor one that leaves him out of position, so you may still have a chance to win the **rally**.

Bend down low to play a reverse-angle shot •

• *Be prepared to leap forward in case your opponent plays short*

SKILL

6 THE BOAST

Playing off the side wall first gives you attacking and defensive possibilities from both the front and back of the court

BOAST STANCE

Use the **boast** shot to either attack or defend. You must strike the ball with pace into the side wall so that it flies to the front. Adopt a similar stance to that for the **drive,** but face the back. This allows you to get your racket behind the ball in order to send it into the side, and from there to the front. The ball has to travel around two or three walls, so as well as using pace, you need to hit upward. If you hit the ball "flat", it will go into the **tin.** To help generate power, face toward the back-of-court, turning forward as you hit.

THE HIT
Play the ball hard into the right-hand wall. Even a shallow, upward angle will be exaggerated by the rebound on the side wall, so aim low to prevent the ball from bouncing into a position favorable to your opponent.

• **RACKET**
Angle your racket upward to direct the ball around two or three of the walls.

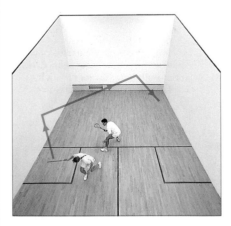

KEEP LOW
Keep the ball low to stop it from coming out of the front corner (bl). It should either die in the **nick** or be difficult to return. Hit with pace to force your opponent to move quickly.

ATTACKING BOAST

When you are positioned in front of your opponent, a **boast** to the front corner can cause problems for your opponent by making him travel from the back- to the front-of-court. Even if you are behind him, you can still play an attacking boast if it sets up nicely in front of you. For this to work, aim for the **nick** on the opposite side of the court. No matter how good your opponent's position, the ball will be almost impossible for him to return. Your shot may miss the nick and yet still be sufficiently difficult for your opponent to deal with. This allows you to regain the initiative as your opponent will be out of position.

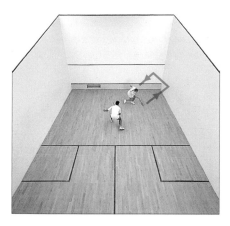

TICKLE BOAST

The tickle **boast**, as its name suggests, is a delicate shot designed to drop low at the front-of-court – like a **drop** shot played off the side wall first. To keep the ball away from the center, aim for the angle made by the front wall and the side wall. Play this shot firmly.

SIDE WALL
To carry the ball around the corner, play it firmly onto the side wall. This shot must be played with more pace than a **drop** shot, to give it sufficient height to reach the front.

DEFENSIVE BOAST

Whenever the ball has gone too far to allow a **volley** or **drive** shot, retrieve the situation with a defensive **boast**. You may have to play this shot when you are at full stretch or on the run, so balance is crucial. Hit upward with pace to get the ball to the front of the court. As soon as you have played it, turn to face the front and recover the T in preparation for the next shot.

BACKHAND RETRIEVE
Backhand retrieve **boasts** are useful when your opponent is trying to intercept a **drop** or down-the-wall shot. Aim for the **nick** to turn your defense into a dangerous attack.

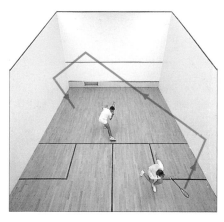

THREE-WALL BOAST
When **boasting** from the corner, aim higher to ensure you reach the front wall. Angle the shot so that it hits the opposite side wall after the front wall to become a three-wall boast.

Watch out for the defensive boast

ANGLE SHOTS

The walls and the angles they make allow you to choose from a wide menu of shots in order to force your opponent around the court

FRONT-OF-COURT

When you are at the front of the court and your opponent is at the back, play a short shot to make him run the full length of the court, or pin him **deep** with a shot to a good **length**. Make use of the walls to cause problems for your opponent by robbing him of the opportunity to intercept. Wall shots exploit the natural angles of the court and prevent you from becoming predictable.

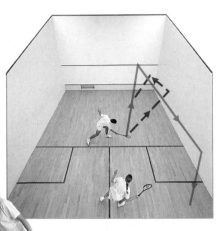

Be aware of your opponent when you select your shot

FOREHAND OPTIONS
There is a useful range of forehand options. The down-the-wall shot (bl) should hit the side wall above the service box, and then bounce in the back corner. This makes the **volley** hard to play and keeps your opponent on the defensive. If your opponent is standing at the back of the court, the tickle **boast** (pl) (see p.55) may be appropriate.

BACKHAND OPTIONS
Give your down-the-wall shot (bl) enough height to reach the back of the court via the side wall, without offering your opponent a chance to **volley**. Don't hit the ball too hard or it will bounce off the back wall to make an easy return.

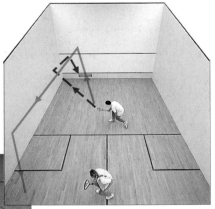

*Use **disguise** to keep your opponent guessing about which shot you are going to play*

BACK-OF-COURT

When you are behind your opponent on the court, use the side wall to gain yourself some time to get into a better position. **Drop** shots can be risky, so only play one if you are confident of success. Usually, a shot across-court or down-the-wall – using the side wall to keep the ball out of your opponent's reach – would be the sensible choice. It is crucial to get height and width to stop the making of an interception that would probably lose you the **rally**.

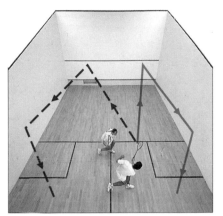

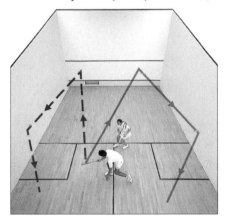

FOREHAND FROM THE BACK
Hit the straight forehand from the back of the court with pace, to force your opponent to the back. To prevent an interception, aim for the side wall, well above the service box (bl). The ball should bounce as near to the back-wall **nick** as possible. Recover the T as your opponent tries to make the return.

BACKHAND ACROSS-COURT
The backhand played from the back, across the court (bl), must be hit with sufficient force to reach the opposite back corner. This gives you time to move forward to the T, while simultaneously forcing your opponent into a defensive situation. Angle the ball into the side wall to prevent a **volley** interception.

MASKING YOUR INTENTIONS

Deception is an effective weapon to use when trying to outwit your opponent in the physical game of chess that is played out on the squash court.
The two keys to achieving **disguise** are:
• Making last-minute adjustments to your classic stance and swing. If you prepare for a powerful **drive**, for example, you can still play delicately by slowing your swing at the last moment and using a **flick** of the wrist to send the ball high to the back of the court, or to drop it short.
• Control – get your balance right and move smoothly. Use your body to mask intentions. Subtle changes of direction and emphasis, together with a good knowledge of the uses of the angles and side walls, will give you an impressive repertoire of shots. Plan out each shot carefully.

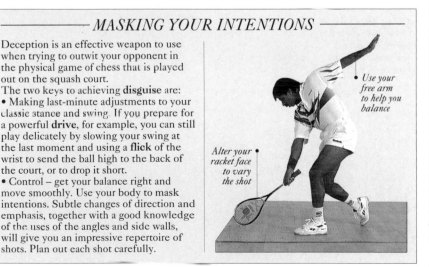

• *Use your free arm to help you balance*

Alter your racket face to vary the shot

7 POSITIONING

Definition: *Finding the areas from which to play winning squash*

A SQUASH COURT is only 32ft (9.7m) long and 21ft (6.4m) wide, but it can seem much larger if you are at the back of it when your opponent plays a **drop** at the front. You may cover the distance, but your energy will be seriously sapped. Remember, the best position to adopt as soon as you have played your shot, is back on the T.

OBJECTIVE: To gain a commanding position from which you can reach all parts of the court quickly. *Rating* •••••

DOMINATING THE COURT

Squash, like the game of chess, is a battle for positional advantage, but in this game, the winner is also able to dictate the speed and style of play

REACH

It is often far better to reach for the ball than to run toward it, as by the time you have got into position, it may be too late to make the stroke, and you will have used up valuable energy. The further you stretch, the more chance you have of making the return. Suppleness and balance are the two key attributes needed for this skill.

• ARM
Use your free arm for balance when you reach low with your racket arm.

• EYES
When waiting, watch to see where the ball is likely to go. Move into position early.

• LEGS
Extend your legs, but remain anchored so that you can push off for the next shot.

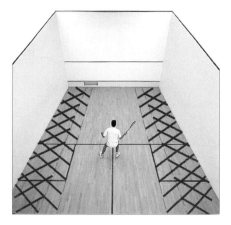

ACTION AREAS

Avoid playing shots that allow your opponent to hit the ball while he is in the middle of the court – the easiest position from which to win the **rally**. The majority of good squash is played near the side walls. The better the player, the nearer the wall most of the action will be. A central standpoint is essential to play this level of game. From this ready position, you are able to reach into each of the corners and intercept any down-the-wall **drives**.

SERVICE BOXES
Imagine that the sides of the service boxes extend to the front and back of the court. Virtually every shot should bounce between these lines and the wall – within the shaded areas. The nearer to the wall your shots land, the harder it will be for your opponent to make a return. Avoid hitting into open-court.

START FROM THE T
By always starting from the T, you should be able to reach the ball in just two or three steps, no matter which part of the court your opponent plays into. You must concentrate on returning to the T after every shot until it becomes almost a reflex action. Both of you will want to occupy the T, so get there first.

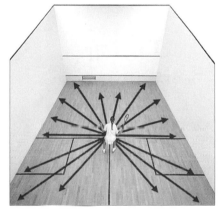

MONOPOLIZING THE COURT

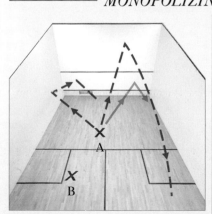

Player (A) will capitalize on player (B)'s position

THE BEST ATTACK
A strong opponent, player (A), will sense when you are in a poor position, player (B), and exploit the situation by sending the ball further away from you (bl). You may manage to return the next shot, but you will almost certainly be forced into a far worse position from which your chance of recovery is extremely slight.

THE BEST DEFENSE
If you are stranded at the back of the court, (B) there are a number of options open to the attacker (A), in both the opposite front corner (bl) and rear corner (pl). It is vital that you recover the initiative. Your best option is to play a defensive shot, such as a **lob**, and recover the T while your opponent makes the return shot.

IMPORTANCE OF THE T

*The T junction, where the **half-court line** meets the **short line**, is the most advantageous position to be in for any shot during the **rally***

WAITING ON THE T

There are two players, but there is only one T, so the battle to gain positional advantage is crucial. You can defeat a player who hits the ball harder than you, just so long as your positioning allows you to intercept **drives** with shots that drop short or **float deep**. It is inevitable that you will sometimes have to move away from the T. At this point, it is vital to return with a shot that forces your opponent to move from the T as well. Think of each stroke as having three components: the preparation, which involves moving to, or stretching for, the ball; the hit; and the recovery, which involves going back to the T.

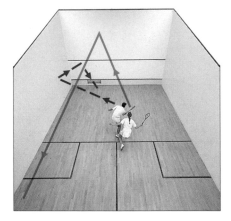

HIT TO THE BACK
When your opponent is "breathing down your neck", play the ball as far from the T as you can. Play a shot to the back with width, pace, or height (bl) to avoid the interception.

• RACKET
Get your racket under the ball to play the defensive return that can force your opponent off the T.

EYES •
When on the T, check over your shoulder for your opponent's position.

RACKET •
Hold your racket well up, in preparation for possible interceptions.

LEGS •
Keep your legs and hips facing forward as you look over your shoulder.

RECOVERING THE T

Your shot is not fully complete until you are back on the T. Assume that your shot will be successful and get ready for the next phase of the **rally**. If it is successful, but you have not recovered the T, your opponent may play a shot that you are unable to return because of poor positioning. Keep your movements smooth – if you lose your rhythm, your balance will suffer and you will be "wrong-footed" by your observant opponent.

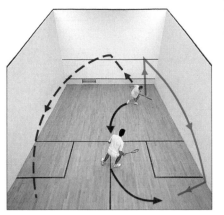

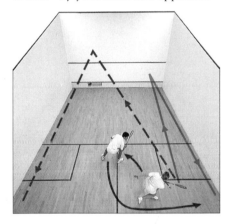

SHORT-BALL OPTIONS
When you have to deal with a **short ball**, it is advantageous to hit it to the back-of-court so that you can return to the T while the ball is traveling. Aim down-the-wall (bl) or across-court (pl) and get away from the front wall – if you are hit by a ball that would otherwise have hit the front wall, you lose the **rally**.

CORNER SHOT
When you have been forced into the back corner, the best option is to play down-the-wall (bl) to regain the initiative and recover the T. This shot must be hit with pace to avoid an interception by your opponent, and should finish near the right-hand corner to force your opponent off the T.

DOMINATING THE COURT

CONTROL THE RALLY
To gain and maintain control of the **rally**, you need to be "fleet of foot" and "sure of arm". You have to be able to always reach the ball, hit it accurately and, if necessary, with power, and then return to the T. You must also be able to play **lobs**, **drives**, and **drops**, and be aware of how the **boast** can help you in certain situations.

TAILOR YOUR GAME
Most importantly, tailor the game to match the skills of your opponent. If your **drops** are always returned, stop using them. If your **drives** set up **volley** interceptions, use another tactic. Assess your opponent's position and choose the appropriate shot. For example, if (A) is on the T, (B) should play to the opposite back corner (bl).

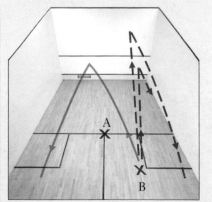

Play the shot as far from your opponent as possible

SKILL
7

INTERFERENCE

Fast sports in confined spaces bring the risk of injury, but the rules of squash are designed to ensure that your game is safe and enjoyable

ILLEGAL SWING

Many injuries are caused when one player is hit by the other's racket. To reduce this risk, the rules state that it is illegal for a player to follow-through in such a way as to endanger their opponent. Remember that both players share the responsibility of ensuring safe play. Think about the type of shot your opponent is about to play and move around him so that he has enough room to make a full swing and follow-through.

• **ARM & RACKET**
During a full follow-through, the length of your arm and racket together is about 4ft (1.2m) – make sure your opponent is a safe distance away from your racket.

• **POSITION**
Don't tempt fate by standing too close to your opponent – it is you, not he, who will get hurt.

• **RACKET**
To complete a full backhand follow-through, keep the racket high and hold your wrist firm.

COMPACT STROKE

Excessive follow-throughs are the consequence of trying to hit the ball with power. In this respect, they are not only illegal but can be counter-productive, since a wild slash at the ball is likely to be poorly timed and will also fail to generate as much pace as desired. If your follow-through is not controlled, the accuracy of the shot will also suffer. Keep your swing smooth by pressing (see p.27) the ball on impact and sweeping through the stroke until your racket is vertical.

OBSTRUCTION

During a **rally**, both players focus on the ball and on returning to the T in preparation for the next shot. Inevitably, they will sometimes get in each other's way. A rally may have to be replayed if the **obstruction** was unavoidable. However, if you are seen not to have made a reasonable effort to get out of the way, the point will be awarded against you.

RACKET •
Obstruction, as well as physical contact, occurs when you cannot complete a full swing for fear of striking your opponent.

MOVEMENT

The direct route to the ball may be obstructed by your opponent, but it is important to make a real effort to go around him. It is unsporting to appeal for **obstruction** when it is clear that you could have played the ball.

RACKET •
If you have to move around your opponent in order to reach the ball, keep your racket well clear of him.

GO FOR IT
Make a genuine effort to reach the ball. It is important to try so that the **obstruction** is clearly evident. If you ask for a **let** on the basis that an obstruction could have happened, you might not be awarded one.

SKILL

8 THE SERVICE

DAY 2

Definition: *The first shot of a rally played from the service box*

SQUASH IS NOT LIKE TENNIS – there are very few **service** aces. The best you can hope for with a good serve is that your opponent will find it difficult to return, giving you an early advantage in the ensuing **rally**. Good serves rely on pace and accuracy in order for the ball to reach the side wall and, from there, the back-of-court. Once there, it is unlikely that an attacking shot will be made. Variety is the key to preventing your opponent from anticipating your serve.

OBJECTIVE: To force your opponent onto the defensive. *Rating* ••••

SERVING TO WIN

The serve is the only occasion in the game where you have the time and space to play exactly the stroke you want – take advantage of it

BACKHAND

Using the forehand serve from the forehand box can put you at a disadvantage, because you need to have your back to the receiver and must then turn to reach the T. However, you can solve this problem by using a backhand serve. It is a difficult shot to play and only really allows you to **lob**, but it is well worth having in your repertoire so that you can vary your attack.

• **EYES**
Keep your eyes on the ball as you press it (see p.27) upward.

RACKET •
Open the racket face and hit the ball from underneath. Aim high.

• **THE THROW**
Throw the ball clear of your body to enable you to make an unimpeded, full swing.

FEET •
To be legal, your left foot must stay in the service box until the serve has been completed.

PRINCIPAL SERVES

Bring a number of serves into your repertoire so that your game is never predictable. Vary **drives** with delicate **lobs** and combine the two to "kiss" the side wall at the most awkward point – just behind the service box. Never angle your serve so that it travels toward the side at an acute angle. If it does, it will come into court where your opponent can make an easy return. The ball should finish within 2ft (60cm) of the back wall.

• RACKET
Angle the racket head to direct the ball across-court.

SMASH
Aim hard and low for the **nick** behind the service box. Occasionally, try speeding the ball down the middle to catch out your opponent.

• RACKET
Make contact with the ball once it is at head height.

WRIST •
Adjust your wrist according to the shot. Use a **flick** to give it pace.

SEMI-LOB
Play the shot firmly, but with a slightly open racket to lift the ball. Hit correctly, it should "kiss" the side wall, bounce off the back, and "die" behind the **service** position.

LOB
A **lob** can be unplayable for your opponent if the ball bounces high against the side wall to land gently in the back corner. Keep the ball close to the side wall to avoid a **volley** return.

SERVICE RETURN

SKILL
8

*A well-executed **service** return can
offset the most accurately played serve*

RECEIVING

Just as a good serve can help dictate
the outcome of a **rally**, so the quality
of the return can determine who gains
the upper hand. Total concentration
is necessary when receiving, since the
server has the time and opportunity to
place the ball where he desires and at
his chosen pace. Position yourself just
behind the service box and watch your
opponent for clues about the type of
serve he is about to play. Always react
quickly and play an attacking **volley**
return whenever possible.

SHOULDERS
Loosen your
shoulders to allow
for a forehand or
backhand return.

RACKET
Hold the racket
head well up and
out in front of you,
in readiness to
return the shot.

KNEES
Keep your knees bent
ready to propel you to
your next position.

POSITION
Stand 2ft (60cm)
behind the service
box, with the leg
that is nearest the
middle of the court
on an imaginary
continuation of the
edge of the box.

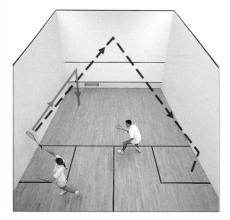

THE KILL
To play the **kill** into the left-hand corner,
volley the ball down the side wall (bl). Aim
above the **tin** to allow a margin for error.

BACKHAND VOLLEY

The **volley** return can be particularly
effective if played before the ball hits
the side wall. Since the shot is played
so quickly, the server has less time to
return to the T and, therefore, is quite
likely to be caught out of position. The
backhand volley is difficult to master,
so the temptation may be to let the
ball drop and attempt to play a **drive**,
but then the advantage will lie very
much with the server. A volley, on the
other hand, opens up a great range of
options, such as a low, straight **kill,** a
down-the-wall shot, a cross-court **deep**
to the corner, and a cross-court **nick**
shot, all of which could win the **rally**.

FOREHAND ATTACK

Even if you don't have a chance to play the **volley** before the serve hits the side wall, you can still play into the front, right-hand corner if the ball rebounds in a position that is clear of the side and back walls. Alternatively, you could try **boasting** the ball to the front, right-hand corner. Either way, the server will have to leave the T in order to make the return, which will give you the opportunity to gain the upper hand. If you are confident at playing volley shots and so are taking most serves before they bounce, it can be effective to let the occasional serve just drop. This will prevent the server from anticipating your response.

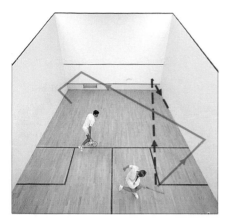

HARD & LOW
Play your shot hard and low into the side wall to send the ball to the opposite front corner (bl). Your shot should ideally land safely in the **nick** or, at least, close to it.

FOREHAND DEFENSE

When your opponent delivers a good serve, you may be forced to play on the defensive. Aim to keep the ball in the air for as long as possible and to force your opponent **deep** to the back of the court. This gives you time to recover your position, and should also negate any advantage your opponent has secured. With your opponent at the back-of-court, play a shot down the right-hand side, or a **skid boast** to land in the opposite back corner.

Hit hard and upward into the side wall

HIGH BOAST
Counter a **deep** serve with a high **boast** that skids off three walls to reach the opposite back quarter (bl). Play upward and with power, to give the ball trajectory and momentum. Recover the T after playing the shot. Don't stand and watch.

• *Remain in the "ready" stance as you check over your shoulder to see what your opponent is up to*

9 RALLYING

Definition: *The series of shots played in the battle for supremacy*

NOT EVERY SHOT YOU PLAY will be an instant winner. If your opponent plays a strong shot and gets into a good position, your only option may be merely to keep the **rally** going. However, if you are forced onto the defensive, your only hope then may be to recover with a shot that restores the status quo. It is a mistake to try to win the rally with every shot you play: you will make far too many errors. Rather, you should continue rallying on the defensive until a definite opportunity emerges for you to attack.

OBJECTIVE: To know which shot to play and when. *Rating* ••••

RALLY YOUR FORCES

*Acquire a repertoire of solid shots to enable you to participate in a lengthy **rally** and force your opponent to play on the defensive*

REACHING

The fewer the shots that get past you, the longer you will be able to stay in the **rally**. Reach for as many shots as you can while remaining on the T, and recover the "ready" position as quickly as possible. It is a good idea to practice playing a range of shots, using an extended stance from the T.

• **ARM**
Use your free arm to maintain balance as you play, and to help you recover the "ready" position in preparation for your next shot.

• **STRETCH**
Always try to avoid surrendering the T to your opponent. Whenever possible, reach for the ball, rather than moving away from the T.

ANTICIPATION

When you are positioned on the T during a **rally**, your opponent will try to move you off it by playing into the corners. Try to anticipate where your opponent is about to place the ball, so that you can begin to move a fraction of a second quicker. This enables you to make a better preparation, and possibly create an opportunity for the **volley** interception. Bear in mind that players good at **disguise** can send you running in the wrong direction.

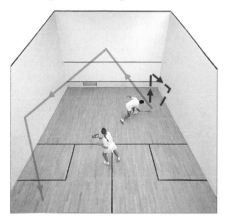

FRONT CORNERS
When your opponent is in front of you, it is difficult to see, and therefore judge, which shot they are about to play. You should be poised on the T, ready to move forward if they play a **short ball** – for example, with a tickle **boast** (see p.55) (bl). Don't always run to the ball – try to reach for it instead.

BACK CORNERS
A skilled opponent may try to outwit you by using the walls to send the ball to the back of the court. If the shot comes across-court, be alert for the opportunity to intercept it (bl). If the shot is well played, you will have to move toward it, but whenever possible try to reach for the ball rather than stray from the T.

PRESSURE

If you manage to succeed in forcing your opponent into the back corner, your position on the T should allow you to create a winning opportunity. You could have to deal with a cross-court shot, but your opponent may refrain from playing one as it can be risky. It is more likely that you will be faced with a shot down the side wall, which your opponent hopes will force you into the corner. Once you know this is the shot being played, intercept with a **drop** volley or a cross-court **nick** shot. This will force your opponent onto the defensive.

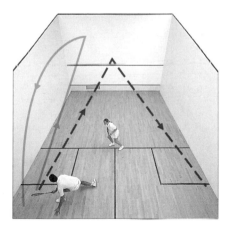

INTERCEPTION
Keep pressure on your opponent by looking to intercept the down-the-wall shot (bl).

SKILL 9

CALLING THE SHOTS

*In every rally, you must think of ways to gain the upper hand –
always plan several shots ahead to outwit your opponent*

EYES
Watch your opponent
for clues as to the
type of shot they
plan to play.

CONCENTRATION

Victory in a **rally** is often determined by one player snatching the fraction of a second that allows him to prepare for a winning shot. Time is gained by getting into a good position, watching what your opponent is doing, and then moving promptly to play the appropriate shot. Always return to the T once you have played your shot, and continue to concentrate on what your opponent is doing.

Don't turn around to watch him when he is standing at the back of the court – you will lose your "ready" position – instead, check over your shoulder while maintaining the correct stance.

EYES
Track the ball onto your
racket and change the
angle of the racket head
at the very last moment.

SHOT SELECTION

The key to effective **rallying** is to choose the right shot at the right moment. If your opponent is behind you, a **drop** shot may be most appropriate. Alternatively, it may be better simply to play a continuation of shots to the back of the court until a weak return provides you with a winning opportunity. A variety of shots is vital – if you consistently play drops, your opponent is better able to anticipate them. Similarly, if you always aim for the back corners, he will remain at the back of the court.

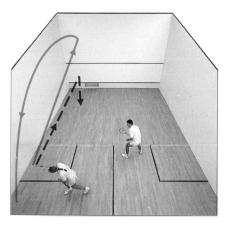

DEFENDING
When "pinned" in the backhand corner with your opponent positioned safely on the 'T', a down-the-wall return to a **length** is a classic **rallying** stroke to play (bl). Get the ball as close to the side wall as possible to make the interception more difficult and land the shot **deep** in the corner to make it harder to **drive**.

ATTACKING
Loose shots played by your opponent can be punished with attacking strokes. If a shot to the forehand corner is high and clear of the wall, it can offer a **volleying** opportunity that might allow you to **kill** the **rally** in the front corner (bl). Play a volley whenever possible to catch your opponent out of position.

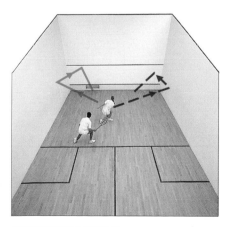

REVERSE ANGLE
Use the forehand **reverse angle** (bl) to send your opponent in the wrong direction.

SEIZE THE INITIATIVE

When your opponent is beginning to dominate the **rally**, you have two options: play a defensive stroke that will give you time to recover the T, or play an attacking shot that could win you the rally. By mixing both types of shot in your strategy, you double your chances. Remaining on the defensive means that you will only win if your opponent makes a careless mistake. Combine low-risk, attacking shots with defensive ones to gain the initiative.

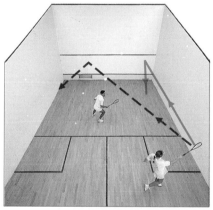

FIND THE WINNER

There are two ways to win the **rally**: either wait for your opponent to make a mistake, or play an outright winner instead. Winners are not easy. If they were, everybody would play them all the time. It is often much wiser to rally effectively until a definite opening arises. At the highest standards, rallies can last for many minutes as players probe each other's defenses in search of a weak return. A popular tactic is to move your opponent from the front- to the back-of-court, using alternate long and **short balls**, in the hope that he misjudges the return.

AFTER THE WEEKEND

After learning the rudiments of squash, start putting them into practice

NOW YOU HAVE MASTERED THE BASIC SKILLS of squash, the best way to improve is to play frequently, against a range of partners. Join a private squash club or local leisure center that runs a "ladder" system or league, where you can regularly play people of a similar ability. Every player you meet will have different strengths and weaknesses, so every game you play should widen your experience and help you to put your technique to better use. Treat each game seriously: get to the court in plenty of time; don't neglect your warm-up routine; and give maximum effort to the game. It is not fair, either to your opponent or to yourself, to play in a half-hearted fashion. Occasionally, in either your league or a tournament, you will come up against someone who is much better than you. This kind of match can teach you many valuable lessons about fitness, stroke selection, timing, and positioning. Concentrate on the factors that enabled the other player to win. If you do get thrashed, don't be depressed – everybody has to learn the game. If you play regularly, you should soon start winning more games than you lose.

PROFESSIONAL ADVICE

Watch and learn from better players.
A professional coach can identify your
weaknesses and point out mistakes in
your techniques. Listen to the advice
you are given, remember it, and then
incorporate it into your next game.

PLAYING FOR LIFE

Sensible training and healthy eating promote good squash playing

•

NOW YOU HAVE MASTERED the rudiments of squash, it is important to find out how you can help your body to cope with the demands the game will place upon it when you play regularly. Playing squash will make you fit, but you should help to reduce the chance of injury or early exhaustion by respecting your body. If you smoke – stop. Don't drink too much alcohol. Eat a healthy, nutritious diet. Get plenty of sleep to allow tired muscles and joints to rest. These measures should help you to improve your physical well-being as well as your attitude to life in general.

AVOIDING INJURY

Never play squash if you feel ill or if you are troubled by an aching joint – you will only make matters worse. For example, if you have a cold, your body will be weak and so will be unable to recover from the exertion. If you have a painful joint, squash will aggravate the problem. Playing while you are not fully fit will, in the long run, only delay your ability to play further.

SHOULDER •
Violent swings can rip cold muscles in your shoulder, neck, and upper back.

LOWER BACK •
Reaching for low shots or stretching for high balls can pull your lower back muscles.

CALF •
Hamstrings can rupture when stretching for a low shot.

— TREATING INJURY —

A dull, mild ache is probably a minor muscle pull, which will heal naturally if you rest the limb for a while. However, a sharp pain in a muscle indicates a tear, which may be accompanied by internal bleeding. Apply a cold compress as soon as possible to stop the bleeding. Seek proper medical attention immediately.

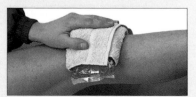

A cold compress stops internal bleeding

STOP THE GAME
Don't play on if you suspect that you have injured yourself. Even with a minor injury, give the muscle every opportunity to rest.

KEEPING FIT

A squash match can last for anything up to two hours, so players need to be fit. A sure way of developing stamina is by taking regular aerobic exercise, which, as well as improving muscle tone, improves the body's capacity to absorb oxygen, so enabling your body to work more efficiently. The best forms of aerobic exercise are brisk walking, jogging, and swimming. Exercise only becomes aerobic after 12 minutes, so you must continue for at least 20 minutes. Aim to include aerobic exercise three times a week.

WORKING FOR FUN
Working out in a gym is an enjoyable way to develop all-round fitness. However, large muscles impede mobility, so don't overdo it.

YOUR DIET

You rarely see an experienced squash player who is overweight. This is due in part to exercise, but diet is also significant. An athlete needs plenty of calories, but they must be obtained from the right sort of food. Fatty and sugary foods such as biscuits, pastries, cakes, sweets, fried food, and dairy products should be avoided, or at least limited. Preference should always be given to foods that are low in fat and high in carbohydrates, vitamins, and fiber. These foods include fish, vegetables, fruit, white meat (without skin), grains, brown rice, pasta, and bread.

Fruit contains valuable vitamins and minerals

Citrus fruits are especially rich in vitamin C

Vegetables abound with essential vitamins

Fish is high in protein and low in fat

Eggs are a good source of protein

Pasta is high in carbohydrates for slow-release energy

Milk is rich in calcium

Grains provide plenty of fiber

IMPROVING THROUGH COMPETITION

You will play better by playing better players

IT IS BEST TO AVOID PLAYING the same opponent all the time, because you will quickly get to know each other's game inside out, and so will find it extremely difficult to develop your skills. Play as many people as you can by joining leagues and competitions. This will expose you to different ways of playing the game, and provide you with ideas on how to improve your technique. Don't worry about getting beaten. In the early stages, it is almost inevitable!

JOINING A CLUB

Squash has increased enormously in popularity. There are now many civic sports centers and private clubs where you can play in pleasant surroundings at a reasonable cost. Most clubs and centers offer other sporting facilities too, such as a gym, tennis courts, and swimming pool. As well as allowing you to play squash with different people, joining a club will give you the opportunity to make new friends with at least one interest in common.

R. JONES

B. NESBITT — • If Nesbitt challenges Jones and wins, he goes to the top. Jones must challenge him to win back the top slot

J. MILLS

M. KENNEDY

M. MARKHAM

T. WALLIS

S. ROGERS — • Rogers can be challenged by Blake or Cahalin

L. BLAKE

B. CAHALIN

L. JOHNSON — • Johnson can challenge Cahalin or Blake – a win moves him above the player he has just defeated

D. KELLY

J. WILLIAMS

SOCIAL CLUB
In many clubs, you can relax after your game in the comfort of the bar. Some have viewing galleries, where you can watch others play.

LEAGUE LADDER
Most clubs run a "squash ladder". Such a system is designed to encourage members to play frequently in order to determine who is the best in the club. A typical ladder allows a player to challenge to a match either of the next two players above him on the ladder. If the challenger wins the game, his name is moved above the player he has just beaten.

ADVANCED PLAY

Notice how advanced players make top-level squash look simple. This is because they are fit and strong, they observe the golden rule of recovering the T, and they think about the shots before playing them. It is only when you come up against a player who is much better than you that you realize how important these elements are to playing advanced squash. But don't despair: with practice, determination, and a willingness to learn from others and from your own mistakes, you will continue to reach higher standards.

WINNING & LOSING

Whether you win or lose, just remember that nothing tastes sweeter than victory; nothing tastes more bitter than defeat. The wise player never lets either taste linger for too long.

TOURNAMENTS

The excitement of playing in tournaments will send adrenaline surging through your body. It is possible that nerves will ruin your match; on the other hand, you might thrive under pressure and become a professional competitive player. Either way, if you are good enough to play tournaments, you must take every match seriously. Your opponent will punish a casual approach. Get to the court early, warm up thoroughly, believe in your own ability, and give it your best shot!

• *Tournament cup*

SHARED TRIUMPH

My father is as proud of my achievements as I am honored by his interest and constant faith in me.

TROPHIES

There are a great many competitions for all levels of player, each of which will award a trophy to the winner. If you are fond of silverware, get practicing!

• *Annual champions' shield*   • *Winner of ladder*

RACQUETBALL

Fast and fun for everyone, racquetball is rapidly growing in popularity

RACQUETBALL IS EASY TO LEARN, but extremely difficult to master. You can enjoy the game the first time you play it, and continue playing for a lifetime without ever getting bored. The game's pace is frenetic, because of the lively ball, yet considerable skill and subtlety are required. Beginners develop an immediate love for racquetball because of its simplicity. The large front-wall "target area" is easy to hit, and the generous rebounds can help a novice stay in the **rally**. As skill increases, the methods of winning rallies become ever more sophisticated, with all the subtleties of court, racket, and ball being brought into play. Strategy replaces power as the crucial attribute, rendering mere brute force insufficient to guarantee victory. Like squash, racquetball offers the opportunity for both competitive and recreational play at every level. At all but the highest standard, it is possible for men and women to compete on equal terms, and children love the game because of its straight-forwardness. The game is suited to two, three, or four players, but the rules (see p.83) are relevant to a two-person game. Racquetball is a great way to obtain vigorous exercise in a pleasant, social environment.

A SPORT FOR ALL
Men and women, young and old, can enjoy racquetball. The equipment required is: appropriate shoes and clothing, a racket, a ball, goggles, and a glove. Supplied with these, you can start enjoying the game straight away.

EQUIPMENT

The correct equipment ensures that your game is safe and enjoyable

COMFORT AND SAFETY are the two main considerations when it comes to getting the right equipment for racquetball. It can be a fast and furious game, which means measures should be taken to help prevent injury. It is also important to wear clothing that is suitable for vigorous exercise. As with every sport involving running, shoes are probably the most important item. You can select from a fairly wide choice of rackets and balls, but it is worth buying the best you can afford. Better equipment not only gives superior performance, but tends to last longer and so save you money in the long run.

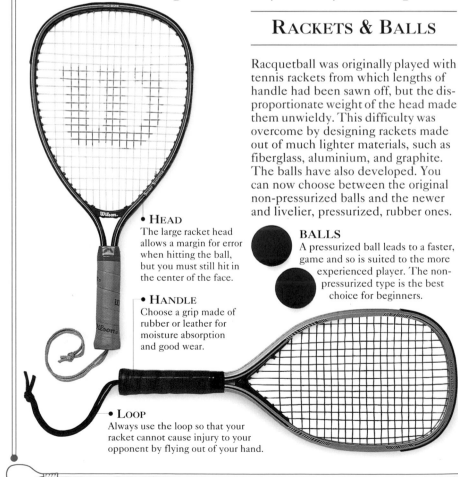

RACKETS & BALLS

Racquetball was originally played with tennis rackets from which lengths of handle had been sawn off, but the disproportionate weight of the head made them unwieldy. This difficulty was overcome by designing rackets made out of much lighter materials, such as fiberglass, aluminium, and graphite. The balls have also developed. You can now choose between the original non-pressurized balls and the newer and livelier, pressurized, rubber ones.

• HEAD
The large racket head allows a margin for error when hitting the ball, but you must still hit in the center of the face.

BALLS
A pressurized ball leads to a faster game and so is suited to the more experienced player. The non-pressurized type is the best choice for beginners.

• HANDLE
Choose a grip made of rubber or leather for moisture absorption and good wear.

• LOOP
Always use the loop so that your racket cannot cause injury to your opponent by flying out of your hand.

CLOTHING

The clothes you wear for racquetball must allow freedom of movement, and be light enough to ensure you don't get too hot. Items that retain moisture will become progressively heavier the more you perspire, and so should be avoided (see pp.10-11). Always make sure that your glove and goggles are comfortable before you start playing – constant adjustment during play is annoying for you and your partner. If your shoes are new, wear them around your home until they fit comfortably.

SHIRT •
Cotton is the best fabric for shirts because it allows moisture to evaporate and so helps to keep you cool.

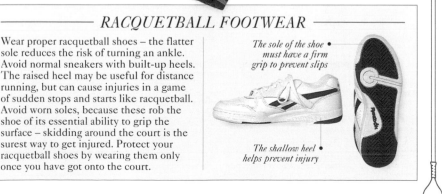

LOOP •
Place your wrist through the loop and gently twist the racket until the loop feels secure yet comfortable.

• Use the headband to adjust the fit

Visors protect • your glasses

GOGGLES
Visors and goggles protect against eye injury. They should fit snugly, but not too tightly. Most have an adjustable strap to allow a comfortable fit.

SKIRT •
Pleated skirts allow women to run, bend, and stretch without being hindered. They also keep the wearer cool.

Fingerless gloves • keep hands cool and improve "feel"

Fingered gloves • offer good protection

GLOVES
Racquetball gloves improve your grip by preventing moisture from your hand reaching the racket. The full-fingered gloves offer the most protection against blisters or chafed, painful skin.

SOCKS •
Cushioned socks help to reduce the risk of blisters. Cotton socks allow your feet to breathe easily.

RACQUETBALL FOOTWEAR

Wear proper racquetball shoes – the flatter sole reduces the risk of turning an ankle. Avoid normal sneakers with built-up heels. The raised heel may be useful for distance running, but can cause injuries in a game of sudden stops and starts like racquetball. Avoid worn soles, because these rob the shoe of its essential ability to grip the surface – skidding around the court is the surest way to get injured. Protect your racquetball shoes by wearing them only once you have got onto the court.

The sole of the shoe • must have a firm grip to prevent slips

The shallow heel • helps prevent injury

COURT & RULES

The dimensions of the court encourage a fast and exciting game

ONE OF THE BEAUTIES of racquetball is the simplicity of its rules, and this is reflected in the design of the court. Viewing galleries at the rear of the court often dictate how much of the back wall and ceiling can be used, but the basic shape of the court remains the same. There are no markings on the walls, and all of the walls and ceiling may be used during play. The markings on the floor are only employed during the serve and the return of serve. The rules are designed to allow a fast-moving game that balances power and skill, and which is safe yet highly enjoyable. The extreme liveliness of the ball means it can travel a considerable distance even when struck only lightly. It will also bounce very high, providing you with more time to play your shot before the second bounce.

DIMENSIONS

The court is a rectangle 40ft (12.1m) long, 20ft (6m) high, and 20ft (6m) wide. The back wall is always at least 12ft (3.6m) high. The floor markings consist of: the **short line**, which is midway down the length of the court and parallel to the front and back walls; the service line, which is parallel to the short line and 5ft (1.5m) from it, going toward the front wall; the service boxes, which are formed by lines connecting the short line and the service line. The service lines are 18in (45.7cm) from, and parallel to, the side walls. The receiving line – an imaginary line – is sometimes marked by two short dashes on either side of the floor.

QUICK & LIVELY
The liveliness of the ball means that most of the action takes place at the back-of-court. An apparently gentle hit can send the ball flying the whole length of the court, and back again.

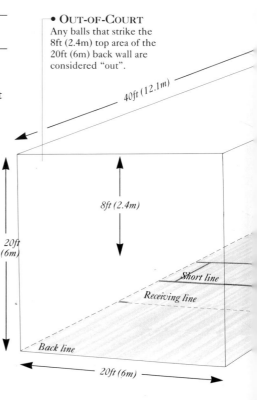

• OUT-OF-COURT
Any balls that strike the 8ft (2.4m) top area of the 20ft (6m) back wall are considered "out".

40ft (12.1m)

8ft (2.4m)

20ft (6m)

Short line

Receiving line

Back line

20ft (6m)

RULES OF RACQUETBALL

Main racquetball rules based on a game for two players. Up to four people can play.

• The server plays from the **service zone**. The ball must bounce once before the server may strike it.
• The server must ensure that the ball hits the front wall first, and then crosses the **short line**, before it touches the floor. The ball is allowed to hit the other walls before the floor.
• The receiver must stand 5ft (1.5m) behind the short line until the ball has crossed it. Neither the racket nor the receiver's body is allowed beyond this line as his opponent makes a return.
• Only the racket head may be used to hit the ball, and the player may make contact with the ball only once for each shot. The racket can be held in one or two hands.

All of the red floor- and wall-markings must be obeyed

• Unintentional **interference**, with the ball, or the other player, results in a "dead ball" hinder being awarded. This results in the point being replayed without penalty.
• Any interference with an opponent's play that could have been prevented, results in an "avoidable" hinder being awarded to the offender's opponent. If the offender was serving at the time, an "out" is awarded, and if he was receiving, a point is awarded.
• Unnecessary delays of ten seconds or more may result in a point being awarded against the offender.
• Unsportsmanlike behavior, such as pushing another player, or failing to make a reasonable effort to get out of the way of either him or his racket, warrants the awarding of a point to the offender's opponent. If three penalties for this type of conduct are given, play stops immediately and the match is forfeited to the "wronged" opponent.

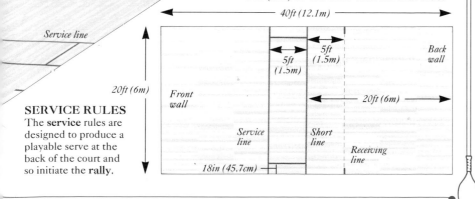

Swings must be controlled

SERVING

The server stands within the **service zone** while he serves to his left or right. The non-server stands behind the service zone while the serve is made. A **drive** serve cannot be played down the side on which the non-server is standing if the server is within 3ft 3in (1m) of the side wall on that side.

Front wall

Service line

20ft (6m)

SERVICE RULES
The **service** rules are designed to produce a playable serve at the back of the court and so initiate the **rally**.

← 40ft (12.1m) →

				5ft (1.5m)	Back wall
5ft (1.5m)				
Front wall				← 20ft (6m) →
	Service line		Short line	Receiving line
18in (45.7cm)				

GRIPS & STROKES

The correct grip and a repertoire of shots are essential for good racquetball

RACQUETBALL, LIKE SQUASH, is a fast game in which the ball travels at great speed around the entire court. To play well, it is necessary to develop a range of forehand and backhand shots so that you are able to respond effectively to rapidly changing situations. It is also important to develop both power and subtlety so that you are able to defend competently and exploit attacking opportunities. The foundation of any stroke is the grip. Make sure that the grip of your racket is comfortable, yet secure, and that you are happy with your glove. Practice alternating between the forehand and backhand grips until the movement becomes almost a reflex action as soon as you decide which shot you are going to play.

BASIC FOREHAND

Most players have a bias toward the forehand: it is the most natural stroke to play. There is a wide variety of forehand strokes from the low-power **drive**, to the delicate **angle shot**, to the defensive **volley**. In every case, the fundamentals are the same: you must watch the ball closely, develop a good backswing, and a full, smooth follow-through. Take the ball when it is in front of you to enable maximum power and control. If you take the ball later, you will have far less time to prepare for your shot, which may result in an unforced error.

GRIP
Shake hands with your racket so that the "V" shape (see p.24) lies on an imaginary line, down the center of the grip. Wrap your forefinger around the grip like a trigger finger.

• **ARM**
When stretching for the ball, use your free arm for balance.

• **LEG**
Keep some flexibility in your legs so that you can move quickly.

• **RACKET**
To allow a full, well-controlled, backswing, the racket should meet the ball in front of your body.

• **FOOT**
Plant your front foot solidly so that you can maintain balance as your body swings into the shot.

BASIC BACKHAND

The backhand is sometimes seen as the weak side, and many opponents try to exploit this by directing most of their shots to that side of the court. It follows then that if you exercise to strengthen your backhand, you have a great advantage over many players. Balance is important, so prepare for the backhand as early as possible. This gives you time to produce a full, smooth backhand and to complete the essential follow-through, which gives you control over direction and pace.

GRIP
For the backhand grip, first hold the racket as if you were about to play the forehand. Then turn the "V" shape toward your body so that it lies along the inside edge of the grip.

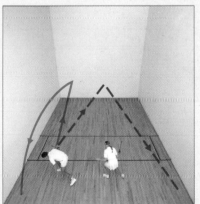

FEET •
Be ready to push off as soon as you have played.

• RACKET
Sweep through the ball and complete the follow-through. Make contact when the ball is in front of your leading leg.

CLASSIC DRIVES

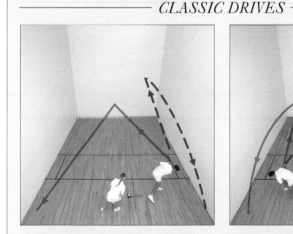

FOREHAND
Use a forehand **drive** to play across-court (bl) or down-the-wall. Angle your shot so that the ball lands far from your opponent and forces her onto the defensive.

BACKHAND
A backhand, down-the-wall shot (bl) is a good attacking shot because, if played with the correct pace and angle, it forces your opponent to return with the backhand.

SERVING

*The opening shot of every **rally** can dictate who wins the point*

IT IS CRUCIAL TO ENSURE THAT your serve conforms with the rules (see p.83), and that it puts you in a strong position for the ensuing **rally**. First, master the basic **drive** serve, then practice a number of alternatives. Inject variety into your serving to prevent opponents from anticipating which serve you are about to use. In certain situations, it helps to be skilled at both attacking and defensive serves. For example, if an opponent is tired, a powerful serve that forces him to run after the fast-moving ball is the best choice.

BASIC SERVE

The basic serve is a low, forehand **drive** to the left or right. It should hit the front wall, close to the floor, and remain just above the floor until it passes the **short line** and bounces. Aim for the side walls to reduce the options available to your opponent. Move to the center after serving.

• RACKET
Prepare your racket and body so that you are ready to spring forward as soon as the serve has been made.

ARM •
Use your free arm for maintaining balance while you are serving.

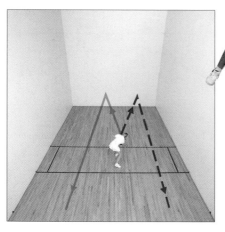

BASIC PRACTICE
Hit the ball hard to see how low you can aim and still make it reach the back of the court without bouncing. Shots to the left (bl) force your opponent into using the backhand.

BASIC SERVE
The serve gives the server time and space to prepare, free of pressure. Exploit this by concentrating on the backswing and follow-through, to ensure correct pace and direction.

ALTERNATIVES

Variations in pace and direction, and
the use of the side walls can expand
your repertoire of serves to provide
a formidable array of opening shots.
Practice on your own rather than
during a match, as mistakes will be
frequent while learning.

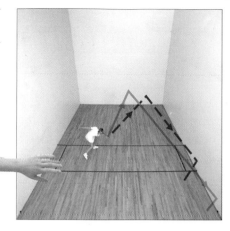

• RACKET
Ensure your
racket makes
firm contact
with the ball.

ANGLE PRACTICE
Hit the **drive** serve so that it hits the side
wall before bouncing. The nearer the back of
the court the ball hits the side wall, the more
difficult it is for your opponent to return.

ANGLE SERVE
The **angle** serve is played low across the
court. Bounce the ball slightly further
away from your body than normal, so that
you have more space to angle your racket.

LOB SERVE
Play the **lob**
serve with the
backhand to force
your opponent
onto the defensive.
Don't overhit, or
it will make an
easy return.

• RACKET
Sweep the racket
upward to give
the ball extra lift.

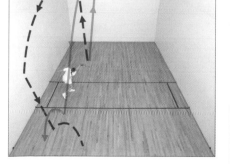

LOB PRACTICE
The **lob** serve should hit the front wall three-
quarters of the way up it. Allow the ball to
bounce high and get your racket under it. It
should bounce twice before reaching the back.

SPECIALIZED SHOTS

A range of shots can be used to exploit the natural angles of the court

RACQUETBALL IS A GAME OF ANGLES. **Rallies** are won when a player sends the ball around the corners and out of the reach of his opponent. The essentials of any winning stroke are direction and pace, but this does not mean simply hitting the ball as hard as you can. Sometimes the slower shot proves more effective.

THE KILL

The **rally** is over if the ball bounces twice, so any shot played low off the front wall is likely to be a winner if it travels away from your opponent. Take your opponent's position into account when selecting your shot. Finding the **nick** between the side wall and the floor produces winners. For a promising **kill**, start with your racket held high and **drive** down to strike the ball when it is close to bouncing on the floor. You cannot be sure your shot will succeed, so always return to the T as soon as possible.

OPPOSITE CORNERS
When your opponent is to your right, play to the left-hand corner (bl). This means that she will have a lot of ground to cover and may be unable to reach the ball in time.

• EYES
Watch to see where your opponent is playing the ball.

RACKET •
Hit low into the corner to **kill** the **rally**.

CEILING SHOTS

The rules of racquetball permit balls to be played off the ceiling. This is useful in defensive situations where you need to force your opponent to the back-of-court, but want to avoid an interception. Don't play a ceiling shot if you are in front of your opponent.

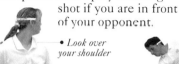

• *Look over your shoulder*

Get under the ball •

UP AND OVER
If your opponent is standing in the **service zone**, bounce the ball over her (bl). From behind the **short line**, aim for a spot on the ceiling, 3ft 3in (1m) from the front wall. The ball will travel from ceiling to front wall, bounce in the front-of-court, and proceed toward the back. The nearer the front the ball hits the ceiling, the **deeper** it lands in-court.

ROUND THE WALLS

The lively nature of the ball means that you can send it across the full diagonal of the court without too much effort. Play this shot to force your opponent to the back, while you recover your position behind the **service zone**.

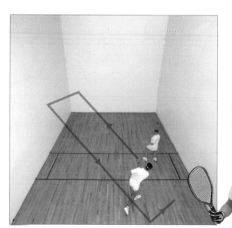

• *Concentrate on your opponent*

Direct the • *ball around the angles*

POWER AND PRECISION
When playing to the back of the court, it is important to deny your opponent the chance to intercept, if possible, so play with pace and ensure that you are accurate. Play off three walls to reach the desired area. Remember to move out of the way on completing your shot.

TACTICS

Brain is as important as brawn in playing quality racquetball

RACQUETBALL IS A TERRITORIAL GAME. If you can secure a strong position and force your opponent into a weak one, you give yourself the opportunity to finish the **rally** with just one well-placed stroke. It is crucial, therefore, to consider where your opponent is, what he is doing, and what he is likely to try to do, before deciding on your own tactics. Adapt to every changing circumstance.

POSITIONING

The best position is in the center of the court, just behind the **short line**, which forms the back of the **service zone**. Like the T on a squash court, this is the ideal place from which to cover any part of the court. Much of the racquetball game is devoted to gaining possession of this area. Once you have obtained control of the center of the court, use your choice of shot to gain the initiative and set the pace of the **rally**.

PLAYING AWAY
One way to stretch your opponent is to hit to the corner furthest from where he is standing. Use the angles of the court to direct the ball to the desired destination.

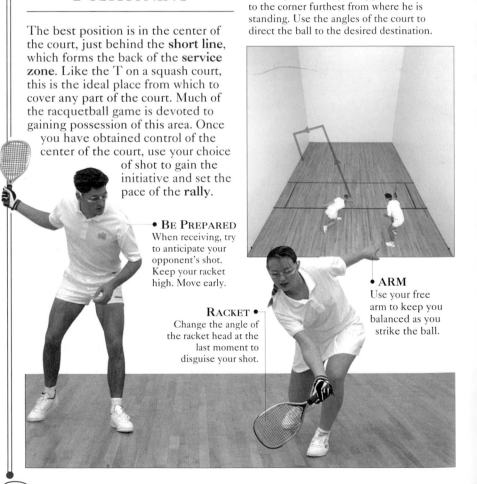

• BE PREPARED
When receiving, try to anticipate your opponent's shot. Keep your racket high. Move early.

RACKET •
Change the angle of the racket head at the last moment to disguise your shot.

• ARM
Use your free arm to keep you balanced as you strike the ball.

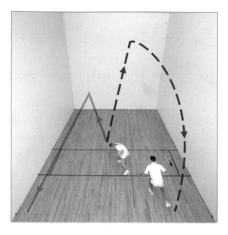

BACKHAND OPTIONS

The backhand can produce powerful **drives** or delicate **lobs**. Choose which to use according to your opponent's position, but inject as much variety as you can. Playing to the front carries a risk of errors, because a low shot might hit the floor first. Play **deep** to keep your opponent on the defensive.

HARD & LOW
A fast ball to the back corner opposite to where your opponent is standing may be a winner if it stays low or finds the **nick** (bl).

CROSS-COURT ANGLES

The ball travels at great speed without bouncing, so you can play it off three, or even four, walls. Such shots change direction several times, making it difficult for an opponent to find the right position to play a return. Use this shot when you want to pin your opponent to the back of the court.

CORNER TO CORNER
Hit hard into the front, right-hand corner and the ball will rebound to the back, left-hand corner (bl), making your opponent struggle.

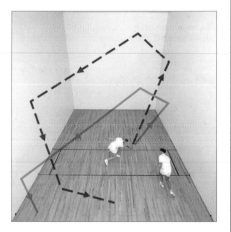

FOREHAND KILLERS

When your opponent is in front of you, turn defense into attack by pinning him to the side wall. He cannot move to the center of the court until the ball has passed him on its way to the front, so if you play at an angle, down the opposite side, he will have to cover a lot of ground very quickly.

FRONT TO BACK
Hit the ball hard to bring it to the back of the court and prevent an interception. Keep the ball low to obtain the second bounce (bl).

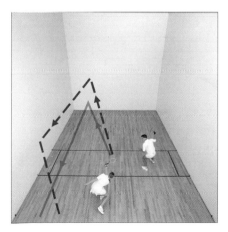

GLOSSARY

Words in *italic* are glossary entries.

A

•**Angle shot** A shot played where the ball first hits the side wall and then the front wall, or vice-versa.

•**Appeals** A player may appeal to the referee or his opponent at the end of a *rally* if he thought that, during the rally, the ball was "down", "not up", or "out".

B

•**Boast** A defensive *angle shot* played off either of the side walls, or the back wall, onto the front wall.

C

•**Cut line** Red wall-marking across the front wall, 1.8m (6ft) above the floor. Serves must hit above this line.

D

•**Deep** When the ball is placed far to the back of the court.

•**Disguise** A technique whereby a player's movements and body position suggest a certain shot is to be played, but in fact an alternative shot is used.

•**Drive** A powerfully played shot, taken low and with width, straight after the bounce (from about knee height), using the forehand or the backhand stroke.

•**Drop** An attacking, return shot that can be played after the bounce and off the *volley*. It is played with very little pace and should, ideally, be aimed just over the *tin* and close to the side wall to land "deadly" in the court or in the *nick*.

F

•**Flick** A shot whose pace and direction are achieved by flicking the racket from the wrist, rather than with a complete backswing and follow-through.

•**Float** A shot played high and with medium power is said to "float" to the back of the court.

H

•**Half-court line** The red floor-marking running from the mid-point of the back wall to the mid-point of the *short line*.

•**Half volley** A shot played a fraction of a moment after the ball has bounced on the floor, but before it rises.

I

•**Interference** Physical contact between players, either person to person, with rackets, or with the ball.

K

•**Kill** An aggressive stroke played hard and low to win the *rally*.

L

•**Length** Any shot that is played *deep* to the back-of-court is described as being played to a length.

•**Let** Where a *rally* has to be played again because a player was impeded.

•**Lob** A delicate shot that sends the ball high and wide over an opponent's head to land at the back of the court.

Backhand **drive**

N

•**Nick** The area of the court where the floor and the sides all join. A ball played into the nick will be difficult to return.

O

•**Obstruction** A player is obstructed when he is unable to reach the ball or swing his racket freely because his opponent is in the way.

•**Out line** The red wall-marking that forms the upper limit of the court on all four walls. A ball that hits this line, or above it, is "out".

R

•**Rally** The period when the ball is in constant play, ending when one player makes an illegal move, hits the ball out-of-court, or fails to make a return.

•**Reverse angle** A shot played across the court into the opposite corner from where the player is standing, which hits the side wall first.

S

•**Scoring** Games are usually played to nine points, with only the server being allowed to score. If the score reaches 8–all, the receiver elects to either play up to 9, or until a two-shot advantage is achieved. Some matches play up to 15, with the server and the receiver having the opportunity to score from each *rally*. At 14–all the receiver decides whether to play up to 15, or until a two-shot margin is reached.

•**Service** The first shot of a *rally*. With one foot in the service box, the server must hit the ball against the front wall, between the *cut line* and the *out line*, to rebound in the receiving, service area.

•**Service zone** The area on a racquet-ball court, between the service line and the *short line*, from side wall to side wall, where the server stands while serving.

•**Short ball** A shot played in such a way that, after the ball hits the front wall, it bounces close to the front wall.

•**Short line** The red floor-marking running parallel to the front wall and stretching from side wall to side wall. It forms the front part of the service boxes, past which the *service* must travel.

•**Skid boast** A ball played to the side wall, high and close to the front wall, which then hits the front wall and lands in the opposite back corner.

•**Slice** Spin added to the ball by slicing the racket beneath the ball. Slice is most effective when playing a *drop*, because the spin causes the ball to rebound toward the floor at an acute angle.

T

•**Tin** The area stretching across the base of the front wall, 19in (0.48m) from the floor. Balls that hit the tin are "out".

V

•**Vibration absorber** A small disc that can be attached to the strings in the middle of the racket face. It helps to absorb vibrations caused when hitting the ball, and prevents them from being transferred to your wrist and arm.

•**Volley** Any return shot that is taken off either the front or side walls before the ball has bounced off the floor. The serve is therefore a form of volley.

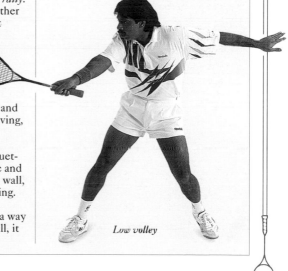

Low volley

INDEX

GETTING IN TOUCH

World Squash Federation
6, Hazelock Road,
East Sussex, TN 34 1BP
Tel: 0424 429245

American Amateur Racquetball Ass.
815 N. Weber
Suite 203,
Colorado Springs, CO 80903

ACKNOWLEDGMENTS

Jahangir Khan, Kevin Pratt and Dorling Kindersley would like to thank the
following for their help in the production of this book:

Klaus Steed and Natalie LeServe for modeling.
Additional modeling by Sgt. Thomas Samms.

Mathew Ward, photographer, and his assistants: Christina Dormier-Valentin
and Martin Breschinski. Emma Kotch and Linda Burns for hair and make-up.
Southbank Squash Club for the squash court.
High Wycombe American Air base for racquetball court and for
lending equipment.

Olympus Sport International, Mr. Hamish Thompson of Reebok (UK) Ltd.,
and Willie Boone of Prince (UK) Ltd. for lending clothing and equipment.

Kevin Williams and Maria D'Orsi for design assistance. Colin Blythe,
Sgt. Thomas Samms, Jane Poynden and Lesley Riley for proof reading.
Hilary Bird for the index. Alistair Wardle and Alison Donovan for squash-court
line artworks. Janos Marffy for color illustrations and line drawings.

Picture Credits: Colorsport; Andrew Cowie p.15 (br),
Stephen Line p.77 (tl & c).
t: top, b: bottom, l: left, r: right, c: center